IT'S MY STATE!

WASHINGTON, D.C.

Terry Allan Hicks

Cavendish
Square

New York

Published in 2014 by Cavendish Square Publishing, LLC
303 Park Avenue South, Suite 1247, New York, NY 10010

Library of Congress Cataloging-in-Publication Data

Hicks, Terry Allan.
 Washington D.C. / Terry Allan Hicks.
     pages cm. — (It's my state)
 Originally published: New York : Benchmark Books, c2007.
 Includes index.
 ISBN 978-1-62712-242-9 (hardcover) ISBN 978-1-62712-501-7 (paperback) ISBN 978-1-62712-253-5 (ebook)
 1. Washington (D.C.)—Juvenile literature. I. Title.

 F194.3.H53 2014
 975.3—dc23

                    2013034185

This edition developed for Cavendish Square Publishing by RJF Publishing LLC (www.RJFpublishing.com)
Series Designer, Second Edition: Tammy West/Westgraphix LLC
Editorial Director: Dean Miller
Editor: Sara Howell
Copy Editor: Cynthia Roby
Art Director: Jeffrey Talbot
Layout Design: Erica Clendening
Production Manager: Jennifer Ryder-Talbot

All maps, illustrations, and graphics © Cavendish Square Publishing, LLC.

The photographs in this book are used by permission and through the courtesy of: Cover (main) Henryk Sadura/Getty Images; cover (inset) Silvia Boratti/Getty Images; p. 5 (top) Leigh Vogel/Getty Images; p. 5 (bottom) © Suzie Banks Photography/Getty Images; pp. 8, 11, 33, 46 SuperStock; p. 9 Jason Reed/Reuters; p. 10 Joel R. Rogers; p. 13 Yoshio Tomii; p. 14 Lester Lefkowitz; p. 15 Karen Hunt; p. 16 Gala; p. 17 James P. Blair; p. 19 Paul A. Souders; p. 20 Katherine Frey/The Washington Post via Getty Images; p. 21 Susanna Raab/Sygma; p. 22 (top) Photo Researchers, Inc: USDA/Nature Source; p. 22 (bottom) David R. Frazier; p. 23 (top) Aaron Ferster; p. 23 (bottom) James Devaney/WireImage/Getty Images; pp. 24, 36, 37, 66 Corbis; p. 27 HIP/Art Resource, NY; p. 28 Richard Cummins/Getty Images; p. 29 Painting by Byron Leister/Washington Historical Society; p. 31 Stock Montage/Getty Images; pp. 32, 38, 41, 52 (top) Bettmann; p. 34 Jahi Chikwendiu/The Washington Post via Getty Images; p. 40 Robert Shafer/Getty Images; pp. 42, 55 Chip Somodevilla/Getty Images News; p. 43 Emily Riddell/Getty Images; p. 44 Jack Novak; p. 48 David Butow; p. 49 Greg Fiume/NewSport; pp. 50, 58 Catherine Karnow; p. 51 Ping Amranand; p. 52 (bottom) Stephen Lovekin/Getty Images; p. 53 (top) Araya Diaz/WireImage/Getty Images; p. 53 (bottom) Gregory Pace; p. 54 Raymond Boyd/Getty Images; p. 59 Alex Wong/Getty Images; p. 60 Lee Snider/Photo Images; p. 62 Ferrell McCollough; p. 64 Envision: Paul Poplis; p. 65 Tom Williams/CQ Roll Call/Getty Images; p. 69 Andrew Harrer/Bloomberg via Getty Images; p. 70 Annie Griffiths Belt; p. 71 Richard T. Nowtiz; p. 72 James Lemass; p. 73 (top) David Freund/Getty Images; p. 73 (bottom) Hisham Ibrahim/Getty Images; p. 74 Art Stein/Zuma; p. 75 Chris Grill/Getty Images.

Every effort has been made to locate the copyright holders of the images used in this book.

Printed in the United States of America.

CONTENTS

A Quick Look at
WASHINGTON, D.C.

Official Flower: American Beauty Rose

The American Beauty was chosen as Washington's official flower in 1925. This lovely, sweet-smelling flower has bright petals in shades from deep pink to red, and a long green stem covered with sharp thorns. Nobody knows exactly where the American Beauty comes from. Some say it was imported from France. Others believe it was first grown in America—maybe even in the gardens at the White House.

Official Bird: Wood Thrush

This charming songbird, which has been Washington's official bird since 1960, can be found in wooded areas in many parts of the city. You are more likely to hear one than to see it, though, because wood thrushes blend in with their surroundings. An adult wood thrush is about 8 inches (20 cm) long, with white and brown feathers. Wood thrushes eat small insects and berries and build cup-shaped nests in trees.

Official Tree: Scarlet Oak

The scarlet oak takes its name from its leaves. They are a bright green in the spring and summer, but turn a beautiful, bright red color in the fall. The bark, which is light brown when the tree is young, changes to dark red as it gets older. Scarlet oaks can grow to a height of 80 feet (24 m), and they are found all over Washington, D.C., in public parks and in people's yards. The district made the scarlet oak, which is sometimes called the red oak or Spanish oak, its official tree in 1960.

Keys to the City

In medieval times, cities often had walls and gates to protect against intruders. Modern cities are no longer guarded in that way, but being presented with the ceremonial keys to the city is a great honor. Washington's ceremonial key was designed by D.C. native John Dreyfuss and is inscribed with the words "Opportunity for All."

National Monuments and Memorials

Washington, D.C., is home to several national monuments and memorials, commemorating important people and events in US history. These include the Washington Monument, Jefferson Memorial, the Korean War Veterans Memorial, and many others.

Official Fruit: Cherry

In 2006, students from Bowen Elementary School proposed making cherries the official fruit of Washington, D.C. The measure was voted on, approved, and signed by the mayor in July 2006. The students chose the cherry because of George Washington's association with the cherry tree and because Washington, D.C., holds a famous cherry blossom festival each spring.

WASHINGTON, D.C.

Highest Point: Tenleytown

Rock Creek Park

16 th. Street

New Hampshire Avenue

National Zoological Park

Washington Cathedral

Michigan Avenue

National Arboretum

Mac Arthur Blvd.

Lincoln Memorial

White House

E. Capitol Street

Vietnam Veterans Memorial Wall

National Mall

Washington Monument

U.S. Capitol

Fort Dupont Park

Pennsylvania Avenue

Jefferson Memorial

Frederick Douglass National Historic Site

Arlington National Cemetery

Bolling Air Force Base

Potomac River

N

W   E

S

The Nation's Capital

One morning in the summer of 1791, George Washington, the first president of the United States, went riding along the Potomac River in Virginia. With him was Pierre Charles L'Enfant, a French-born engineer and architect who had fought at Washington's side during the Revolutionary War. The two men were looking at the place where they planned to build the capital of their new country, the United States of America.

At first, the area did not look very promising. The land close to the Potomac River was mostly swampland, and the areas farther from the river were covered with thick forests. Few people lived nearby. Farms and plantations were scattered here and there. There were only two small towns—Alexandria, on the Virginia side, and Georgetown, across the Potomac in Maryland. Despite all of this, the land was chosen as the grounds for the new capital.

That stretch of land along the Potomac has grown to become one of the world's great cities. It is now home to more than 600,000 people. It is the heart of a larger area with a population of nearly six million people. It is the place where decisions that affect the entire world are made. It is the nation's capital—Washington, D.C.

Quick Facts

Washington, D.C.'s Borders

Southeast	Maryland
Northeast	Maryland
Northwest	Maryland
Southwest	Virginia

All three branches of the federal government, or the government of the whole country, are centered in Washington, D.C. The US president lives and works there in an elegant mansion on Pennsylvania Avenue known as the White House. The Congress meets there, in the US Capitol Building, to vote on the country's laws. The country's highest court, the US Supreme Court, where some of the nation's most important legal cases are heard, is there, too.

Tens of thousands of people stream into downtown Washington, D.C., every day, many of them coming from the city's suburbs to work at government jobs. They are joined by thousands of visitors from across the country and around the world. Some of these "out-of-towners" come to Washington, D.C., to do business with the government. Others come to enjoy all the activities that have made Washington, D.C., one of America's greatest tourist attractions.

The 2-mile-long (3.2 km) National Mall is a central feature in the District.

This photo shows a view of Washington, D.C., from above. You can see the five-sided Pentagon near the bottom of the photo and the Washington Monument near the center.

Quick Facts

People all over the world know the nation's capital as Washington, D.C. The people who live there, though, are more likely to call it "the District" or just "D.C."

Millions of tourists visit Washington, D.C., every year. They are drawn by the city's great buildings and monuments, its beautiful parks and museums, and by its cultural activities. Many come to celebrate America's past but find that present-day Washington, D.C., is every bit as exciting as its history.

The District

Washington, D.C., is different from other American cities, because it does not belong to any state. It is part of a completely separate area, called the District of Columbia—or D.C. The land covers 68 square miles (176 sq km) and is located on the north shore of the Potomac River. It is shaped like a diamond with one of its corners missing. The state of Virginia lies across the Potomac to the south. On the other three sides of the diamond, the District is bordered by the state of Maryland.

The Potomac runs through the heart of Washington, D.C. This great river rises in the Blue Ridge Mountains, in western Maryland. It flows southeast for 285 miles (459 km) and finally empties into the Chesapeake Bay, a large inlet

Many Washingtonians enjoy rowing along the calm waters of the Potomac River.

The Washington Monument is the tallest structure in Washington, D.C.

of the Atlantic Ocean. When the Potomac River reaches Washington, D.C., at the Little Falls in the northwestern part of the district, it is still a fast-moving river that white-water kayakers love to challenge. This section of Washington, D.C., is part of a geographical region called the Piedmont. The Piedmont is an upland plain with plenty of fertile farmland. The Piedmont stretches as far north as Pennsylvania and as far south as Alabama.

By the time the Potomac River passes through the center of Washington, D.C., it has become a quieter, more peaceful stream. This is because this part of Washington, D.C., lies on a mostly flat area called the Atlantic Coastal Plain. This is a low-lying region that stretches along the Atlantic Ocean from New Jersey to Florida. Here, the Potomac River rises and falls with the ocean tides of the Chesapeake Bay.

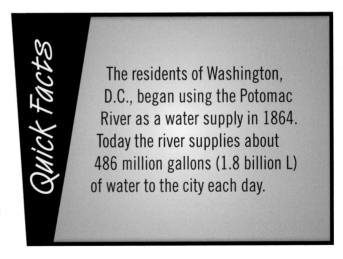

Quick Facts

The residents of Washington, D.C., began using the Potomac River as a water supply in 1864. Today the river supplies about 486 million gallons (1.8 billion L) of water to the city each day.

Other rivers crisscross Washington, D.C., too. All of them flow into the Potomac. The Anacostia River runs south through the eastern part of the district. Rock Creek, a much smaller stream, flows gently through wooded parkland in the northwestern section of the district. There is even a stream that lies mostly underground—Tiber Creek, which was covered over when Constitution Avenue was paved in the late 1800s.

The City

Even though it is the capital of a great nation, Washington, D.C., has few very tall buildings or skyscrapers. The Height of Buildings Act of 1910 limited the tallest buildings to about 130 feet (40 m). In the center of the city is Capitol Hill. The city's main streets spread out from Capitol Hill, like the spokes of a giant wheel. Located on Capitol Hill is the US Capitol Building, home to the legislative branch (the lawmaking part) of the federal government. Many of the nation's most important events take place here. Every four years, for example, the president is sworn in on the Capitol steps. And it is here, inside the Capitol, that US senators and representatives from all the states meet to cast their votes on important issues. Many other buildings are located on Capitol Hill, including the Supreme Court Building and the Library of Congress.

Washington's Neighborhoods

DOWNTOWN:

Many of the most famous sights in Washington, D.C., are in the downtown area, near the Capitol. At the foot of Capitol Hill lies the National Mall. Not to be confused with an indoor shopping mall, the National Mall is a 2-mile-(3.2 km) long park lined with trees. Washingtonians love to come to the Mall to eat lunch, relax in the Sun, and enjoy everything from a brass-band concert to a kite-flying contest.

Halfway down the Mall is the tall column of the Washington Monument. Every year, more than 800,000 people visit this monument. However, in 2011, the monument was closed for repairs after being damaged by an earthquake.

The Capitol is an impressive sight to see—day or night.

About 2 miles (3.2 km) away from the Capitol, on the banks of the Potomac at the western end of the Mall, is the Lincoln Memorial. This huge building, inspired by Greek temples, holds a grand statue of President Abraham Lincoln.

The Mall is lined with beautiful stone and marble buildings, including many of the city's great museums. Some of these museums—such as the National Museum of Natural History and the National Museum of the American Indian—are part of the Smithsonian Institution. The Smithsonian is a group of museums, research centers, and educational institutions, most of which are located in Washington, D.C.

The National Mall is also the site of one of the most moving monuments in Washington—the Vietnam Veterans Memorial. This simple monument is made up of two black granite walls inscribed with more than 50,000 names. These names belong to the brave Americans who are known to have died in the Vietnam War.

The Smithsonian Institution is made up of 19 museums and galleries, a zoo, and nine research facilities. Its collection includes everything from dinosaur bones to spacecraft!

Georgetown is a busy neighborhood filled with homes, stores, and restaurants.

NORTHWEST:

This is the largest part of Washington, D.C., both in area and in population. The Northwest includes the elegant row houses of Georgetown. Many of government officials have homes there. Washington's Chinatown is also found here, as well as the Adams-Morgan area, a place in which many people of different ethnic backgrounds live.

Representatives of dozens of foreign countries work along Embassy Row, which is located on Massachusetts Avenue. This is where the embassies of many countries are located. Embassies are buildings that contain offices for important officials from other countries.

In the spring, residents and visitors stroll along the Tidal Basin to admire the blooming cherry trees.

The John F. Kennedy Center for the Performing Arts is also located in the Northwest, in a neighborhood known as Foggy Bottom. The region got its name because this part of the city's air was once polluted with smoke from factories. The Shaw District, one of Washington's historic centers of African-American culture, is also found here.

The Northwest is also home to Arlington National Cemetery, where more than 285,000 veterans from every war in US history are buried. The most famous grave in the cemetery is probably that of President John F. Kennedy, who was assassinated in Dallas, Texas, in 1963.

SOUTHWEST AND SOUTHEAST:

The southwestern section of the district is a very small area. It has only about 4 percent of Washington's population. The area is mostly used for government offices, including the headquarters of the Department of Transportation.

The southeastern section of the district is a mixed area. There are both large and small homes, as well as national landmarks. One of the landmarks in the Southeast is Cedar Hill, home of the great African-American leader Frederick Douglass. Another area of the Southeast is called Uniontown, which was built

Cedar Hill is the historic home of African-American abolitionist Frederick Douglass.

to provide housing for the shipbuilders who worked at the nearby Navy Yard. Robert F. Kennedy Memorial Stadium, where many of Washington's professional sports teams play, is also found here.

NORTHEAST:

The Northeast is home to several neighborhoods where Washingtonians live. It also has many educational institutions, including Gallaudet University—the only university in the world for hearing-impaired people. Another interesting area in the Northeast is Little Rome, which has more Catholic institutions—such as The Catholic University of America—than any other place in the United States. The Northeast also has public gardens, including the US National Arboretum.

Beyond the Beltway

Washington, D.C., is circled by a major highway called the Capital Beltway, which carries heavy interstate traffic around the city. Many of the people who work in Washington, D.C., actually live beyond the Beltway, in the surrounding suburbs. Washington, D.C., is the center of a heavily populated area that includes large parts of Virginia, Maryland, and even West Virginia. This area, called Greater Washington, is home to almost six million people.

The Natural World

Washington, D.C., has preserved its natural beauty better than many big cities. Most of Washington's main streets are lined with graceful old trees. Some of them are familiar species—or types—that have always grown in the area. These include pin oaks, red oaks, lindens, willows, and sycamores. Other trees in the area are exotic imports from other parts of the world. For example, in 1805, Thomas Jefferson, the country's third president, ordered Lombardy poplars from Italy to be planted along Pennsylvania Avenue. Since then, many other foreign trees have been brought to the nation's capital, including acacias, locust trees, ailanthus (also known as "trees of heaven"), and the beautiful Japanese cherry trees. Every spring, Washingtonians and visitors to the district wait for the Japanese cherry trees to blossom. About 3,750 of these beautiful trees, originally a gift from the city of Tokyo, Japan, line the Tidal Basin.

Nearly 150 parks are scattered across Washington, D.C. These parks are home to a surprising amount of wild plant and animal life. Skunk cabbages and jack-in-the-pulpits grow beautifully in the marshy lowlands along the Anacostia River. Trailing arbutus, bloodroots, golden groundsels, and Virginia bluebells can be seen all over the city. The parks are also home to many kinds of wild birds, including songbirds such as finches, yellow warblers, and thrushes. Birdwatchers can also see blue jays, chickadees, mockingbirds, and mourning doves.

The usual big-city animals, such as gray squirrels, can be found in the district's parks. These squirrels often beg for food from people walking by.

In some places—such as the more remote parts of Rock Creek Park—you might also see foxes, flying squirrels, muskrats, opossums, and raccoons.

However, several of the species once found in Washington, D.C., have been placed on the government's endangered species list. The shortnose sturgeon and the dwarf wedgemussel are both considered endangered. When an animal is endangered, its population in the wild is very small. This is partly because of pollution and because the city has spread out into these creatures' natural habitats. The bald eagle, the national bird, was once considered endangered. However, bald eagles have made a great recovery and were taken off the endangered species list in 2007.

In recent years, Washington, D.C., has worked hard to protect its natural environment. Many of these environmental efforts focus on the rivers that run through the heart of the city. The Potomac was once so badly polluted by waste from factories and sewers that the *Washington Post* newspaper called the river

Traffic on the Beltway can get bad when many commuters are traveling to and from the district.

Nationals Park, located on the Anacostia River, is home to the city's baseball team, the Washington Nationals.

"an open sewer." The fish in the river were badly contaminated by chemicals in the water and sometimes died by the thousands. Beginning in the 1970s, new government regulations began to reduce pollution, and today the Potomac River is a much cleaner, healthier waterway for fish and for human beings. Unfortunately, the Anacostia River is still badly polluted. However, efforts are underway to try to solve this problem.

Washington's Climate

Washington, D.C., has a mostly warm, wet climate. Spring comes early in the district, sometimes as early as late February, when much of the northern part of the United States is still covered with snow.

Summers can sometimes be very unpleasant in Washington, D.C. The city is hot and extremely humid from May until September. The average temperature in July is 78°F (25.5°C), but it can seem much hotter because of the humidity. Humidity is the moisture in the air, which tends to make the air feel damp. Heat waves that pass through the city in the summer can push the temperature over 90°F (32.2°C), sometimes for days at a time. Summers are also very rainy.

An average of 50 inches (127 cm) of precipitation, or rain and snow, falls on the district each year. Most of this is rainfall. This is higher than the national average, which is about 40 inches (102 cm).

Autumn is usually a delightful time in Washington, D.C. The summer's sticky heat gives way to cooler temperatures. The trees in the city's parks blaze with red, yellow, and gold, and the air turns pleasantly cool.

Winter in the district, though, can be difficult and unpredictable, with weather conditions that change quickly. A Washington, D.C., winter is often mild, with average temperatures of 37°F (2.8°C). Warm air coming up from the south may make the district so warm that people walk around in light jackets. Sometimes, though, a storm called a nor'easter passes through, bringing extremely cold temperatures and dumping huge amounts of snow and sleet on the city. When that happens, Washington sometimes shuts down completely, with cars and trucks unable to move on the city's streets.

When it snows, many Washingtonians break out cross-country skis and sleds.

Plants & Animals

Japanese Cherry Trees

Japanese cherry trees are not native to the United States, but today they are grown throughout different parts of the country. The cherry trees surrounding the Tidal Basin were a gift from Japan in 1912. In the spring, the trees bloom with white or pink flowers and the district hosts a National Cherry Blossom Festival.

American Peregrine Falcon

These birds of prey can fly at speeds around 50 miles per hour (80 km/h) and can go as fast as 200 miles per hour (322 km/h) when they are diving. Because of pesticides in the environment, the American peregrine falcon was once severely endangered. Today, though, the birds have made an amazing recovery and were taken off the endangered species list in 1999.

Lombardy Poplars

These tall, graceful trees—named for the Lombardy region of Italy—grow in many parts of Europe and Asia. They first appeared in Washington in 1805, when President Thomas Jefferson had some brought from Italy to be planted along Pennsylvania Avenue. Though it did not originate in the United States, it is one of the country's most popular trees for planting.

Giant Pandas

Pandas are not native to North America, but they have become a symbol of Washington, D.C. These bears live in forests along the mountain ranges in parts of China. Unfortunately, there are only about 1,000 giant pandas left in the wild, and they are considered an endangered species. Special breeding programs have been established to ensure that pandas do not become extinct, or die out. The National Zoo has been home to some of these bamboo-eating bears since 1972.

Sycamores

The sycamore is a type of tree that is native to the Washington, D.C., area and much of the eastern United States. Sycamore trees have delicate, light-colored bark and densely packed leaves that look a little like spread-out hands. The sycamore—which is also called the buttonwood or buttonball—can grow to be more than 100 feet (30.5 m) tall.

Bald Eagles

The bald eagle is the national bird of the United States, so it seems fitting that the majestic birds can be found in the nation's capital. In 2013, National Geographic set up a webcam to let people watch a family of bald eagles living in a tree on the grounds of the Metropolitan Police Academy. Two chicks were born in the nest in March 2013.

From the Beginning

N ative Americans were living in the area that was to become Washington, D.C., as long ago as the Paleo-Indian period, around 11,000–8000 BC. Little is known about the earliest of these peoples, who probably hunted wild animals and also ate wild plants. Archaeologists, or scientists who study the past, digging in Rock Creek Park have found stone weapons and cooking dishes made in about 2000 BC.

By the late 1500s, when the first Europeans arrived in the area, the Potomac River region was home to Native American people called the Piscataway. They belonged to the Algonquian group of peoples, who lived in a huge area that stretched from the East Coast to the Rocky Mountains. The Piscataway were a farming people who lived in small villages and tended crops such as beans, corn, squash, and tobacco. They also used nets to catch fish in the waters of the Potomac and the Anacostia rivers. The Piscataway were often at war with the Algonquians' traditional enemies, the Iroquois, who lived farther north.

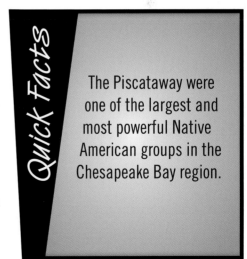

Quick Facts

The Piscataway were one of the largest and most powerful Native American groups in the Chesapeake Bay region.

These young Washingtonians sold newspapers and gum to help support their families.

When the Europeans arrived, the Piscataway had been weakened by years of conflict with the Iroquois. They found it difficult to resist the new arrivals on their land. The Natives also suffered because they caught diseases carried by the Europeans. These diseases had not been present until the explorers and settlers came, so the Native Americans had little immunity to them. By the 1680s, nearly all the Piscataway in the area were gone. Those who had survived moved north to join their old rivals, the Iroquois.

European navigators began to explore the coastal waters near present-day Washington, D.C., in the early 1600s. In 1608, John Smith, who had founded a settlement at Jamestown, Virginia, a year earlier, mapped the Potomac River as far inland as the Great Falls. Smith's map showed many Native American villages along the banks of the river and beyond.

The first European who lived in the area that is now Washington, D.C., was an Englishman named Henry Fleete. In 1632, he built an outpost on the Potomac River. There he traded with the Native Americans, giving them European supplies and tools in exchange for furs. That same year, the English king granted a large area of land called the Maryland Colony to a nobleman named George Calvert, or Baron Baltimore. This new colony included the area that was to become Washington, D.C.

Two years later, in 1634, Calvert's son Leonard—accompanied by "twenty gentleman ... and 300 laboring men"—landed at Chesapeake Bay. They divided the Maryland Colony into huge plantations, called manors. The plantations began growing tobacco, which was then a new and very profitable crop. These plantations made their owners very wealthy. Most of the work, though, was done by slaves brought from Africa. By the end of the seventeenth century, historians believe that about every third person in the Maryland Colony was a slave.

The land along the Potomac River remained mostly farmland until the mid-to-late eighteenth century. The first town in the area, Georgetown, was founded in 1751. This port on the Potomac gave the tobacco growers an easy way to ship their crops to markets in Europe.

This illustration by a European explorer shows natives of the region fishing in the Potomac.

Before Washington, D.C., was built to house the US government, officials met in many different cities, including New York City and Trenton. Carpenters' Hall in Philadelphia housed the First Continental Congress in 1774.

A New Capital for a New Nation

In 1776, the thirteen colonies along the Atlantic Coast declared their independence from Great Britain. Brave colonists fought against British troops and eventually won. The new country needed a capital—a place where its lawmakers could meet. For almost twenty-five years, though, the United States of America did not have a permanent capital. The nation's lawmakers could not agree on a location for a permanent capital. The government moved many times in those years. The Congress met in Philadelphia, Baltimore, and New York City. They also met in a number of smaller towns in Pennsylvania, Maryland, and New Jersey.

They finally turned to someone who was respected by almost everyone— George Washington. General Washington had led colonial troops against the British and had become the nation's first president in 1789. One reason why Washington chose the site on the Potomac River was because it was located almost in the middle of all the new states that lined the Atlantic Coast.

Lawmakers could travel there easily no matter where they lived. The site was also very close to Washington's home in Virginia, so he knew the area well. Washington also decided that the capital should be in a separate district that was not part of any state.

Not everyone was enthusiastic about this location. Thomas Jefferson, who was Washington's vice president, said it was nothing more than "a swamp in the wilderness." Even with this objection, Congress decided in 1790 to build the capital here. They called the new capital Washington in the president's honor. The state of Maryland gave 70 square miles (181 sq km) of land, and Virginia gave another 30 square miles (77 sq km). This section of land was given the second part of its name, which became the District of Columbia, for the explorer Christopher Columbus.

Pierre Charles L'Enfant, seen here, once said that "No nation had ever before had the opportunity of deliberately deciding on the spot where their capital should be fixed."

George Washington called on Pierre Charles L'Enfant to design a city that would become the nation's capital. L'Enfant was a Frenchman who had come to fight on the American side during the Revolutionary War. After the war, he worked as an architect and engineer in New York. L'Enfant spent three weeks exploring the site Washington had chosen. He was helped by two brilliant assistants—Andrew Ellicott, a local surveyor, and Benjamin Banneker, an African American who had been freed from slavery in Maryland.

In his plans, L'Enfant imagined that the Congress would meet in a grand building on Jenkins Hill—later renamed Capitol Hill. The president would live in a great mansion on Pennsylvania Avenue. Many wide streets and avenues would fan out from the hill, and buildings, monuments, and statues would be scattered all over the city.

L'Enfant's plan—and his hot temper—made him very unpopular with the local landowners. One of the landowners was building a house exactly where L'Enfant planned to put a street. L'Enfant had the house torn down. When he did this, the landowners demanded that L'Enfant be fired, which he was. When he left, L'Enfant took his plans with him. Fortunately, Benjamin Banneker was able to reconstruct the plans from memory.

By 1800, the city of Washington was ready for the government to move in. However, it was nothing like the great city it is today. Only one wing of the Capitol was finished, along with a few other government buildings. The city's unpaved streets were choked with dust in dry weather, and when it rained they became a

Many schools, streets, and parks have been named for Benjamin Banneker in honor of his contributions to US history.

sea of mud. People dumped garbage in the streets, and pigs and cows wandered wherever they liked. Fortunately, the government did not really need very much space in those days. In 1800, the government employed only 127 people.

On November 2, 1800, John Adams became the first president to live in Washington, D.C. The White House was not finished when Adams moved in, though. The plaster on the walls was still wet in many places, and many of the rooms were unfinished. The president's wife, Abigail Adams, often hung laundry to dry in the unfinished rooms.

The War of 1812 brought much destruction to Washington, D.C.

Washington at War

The capital was still under construction when the new country went to war for the first time. The War of 1812 was fought between the United States and Britain, mostly over the right of ships to travel freely on the Atlantic Ocean. On August 24, 1814, the British forces attacked and occupied Washington, D.C. British soldiers burned much of the city, including the White House, the Capitol, and the bridge over the Potomac River. The president, James Madison, and his government were forced to flee to Virginia. Only a sudden thunderstorm, which put out many of the fires, saved the city from complete destruction.

Quick Facts

As Washington burned, Dolly Madison and a few White House slaves worked to save valuable and historic artifacts before they were destroyed. One of these slaves, Paul Jennings, was honored by President Barack Obama in 2009.

Washingtonians were determined to rebuild after the War of 1812, and soon the capital was growing again.

In the years after the War of 1812, Congress moved quickly to begin rebuilding the nation's capital. It was during this time that many of Washington's most familiar landmarks appeared. By the end of the 1820s, the White House had been rebuilt and the Capitol was nearly complete. In 1848, construction of the Washington Monument began. The first part of the Smithsonian Institution opened in 1852. This peaceful period of growth lasted only a few decades, though. In the early 1860s, war came to Washington, D.C., again, largely because of an issue that had troubled the country since its beginning—slavery.

Washington, D.C., was an important center of the slave trade. Slaves were actually auctioned off along the National Mall. By 1850, though, the abolitionist

The Peace Conference was held at Washington's Willard Hotel, which still stands today.

movement, which was trying to end slavery across the United States, succeeded in banning the slave trade in Washington, D.C. Slavery still existed in the city, but buying and selling slaves was now illegal.

The slavery issue greatly increased the tensions between the South, where slavery was widely practiced, and the North, where it was mostly against the law. In 1861, the Southern states declared themselves independent, and the Civil War broke out.

The war was long and difficult, and it came dangerously close to Washington, D.C., which was part of the North, or the Union. One of the first major battles of the war was fought at Manassas Junction, Virginia, on July 16, 1861, about 25 miles (40 km) outside of Washington, D.C. The North lost that battle to the South, called the Confederacy, and thousands of wounded men streamed into

During the Civil War, Union troops surrounded the White House to prevent an attack by the Confederate forces.

African-American students do their morning exercises in front of their school.

the district. Throughout the war, Washington's hospitals could not hold the sick and wounded who were filling the city. Many homes, churches, and government buildings, including parts of the Capitol, were used as hospital wards.

On April 14, 1865, Washington, D.C., was shocked by one of the most tragic events ever to take place there. Abraham Lincoln, who was president at the time, was assassinated, or killed, by John Wilkes Booth at Ford's Theatre on Tenth Street. Booth was an actor who had sided with the South. Just days after the tragedy, the Civil War ended when Confederate troops surrendered.

The Civil War changed Washington, D.C., and the country in many ways. The Confederate states were brought back into the Union and slavery was officially abolished throughout the country. Washington's population increased, growing from 75,000 in 1860 to more than 100,000 in 1865. Many of these new Washingtonians were African Americans moving from the South. The free black people of Washington began to play an even more important role in the life of the city.

In the years after the war, a government agency called the Freedmen's Bureau founded schools for black people all over the city. The most famous of these schools was Howard University, which opened its doors in 1867. Today it is considered one of the top historically black colleges and universities in the country. African Americans also began to play a role in Washington, D.C., politics. In 1868, two black men were elected to the city council. This made them the first African Americans ever to hold political office in the city.

In 1871, Washington, D.C., was officially declared a municipal corporation. This meant that the city (including Georgetown) was combined with the county of Washington and the District of Columbia to form a single unit. In 1874, after financial problems left the city deeply in debt, Congress decided that Washingtonians would no longer have the right to run their own city. Instead

In the early 1900s, these young Washingtonians learned how to sew at their all-girls school.

During the Great Depression, a congressman buys an apple from an out-of-work Washingtonian.

of an elected government, Washington was to be managed by three people appointed by the president. One reason for this decision was that some Southern leaders in Congress, who opposed equal rights for African Americans, did not want to see black people gain political power in the nation's capital. Another reason was because some of Washington's elected officials were not wisely using the district's money.

Modern Washington

When the twentieth century began, Washington, D.C., was well on its way to becoming one of the world's great cities. The federal government had grown so much that it now employed more than 25,000 workers. In 1917, the United

States entered World War I. During the war, the government needed more workers. This helped Washington's population to grow, reaching 450,000. During this period and into the 1920s, a great deal of construction was done in Washington, D.C. The Lincoln Memorial was finished in 1922.

Many things had changed in Washington, D.C., but some, such as the economic conditions of the city's black residents, did not. African Americans could enter most public places and ride freely on the city's streetcars. However, jobs and other forms of opportunity were not open to blacks. This was made worse in 1929 when the Great Depression hit. During the Depression the country's economy collapsed. Millions of people all over the country lost their jobs. Many of them poured into Washington, D.C., looking for work. At one point in 1934, almost 40,000 people were arriving in the city every day! In all parts of the country, businesses closed and farms were abandoned. Many people left their homes and moved westward, looking for more opportunities.

Some relief came when President Franklin D. Roosevelt's government created "make-work projects." These projects were designed to give jobs to unemployed people, while also improving the country. Workers repaired roads and bridges all across the country. In the west, many workers were sent to lumber camps to cut down trees. Many of Washington's great buildings, including the Supreme Court Building and the Jefferson Memorial, were completed during the 1930s, putting many unemployed people to work.

The United States entered World War II in 1941, sending soldiers to help fight against Japanese, German, and Italian troops. The war improved the nation's

In Their Own Words

It is sometimes called the City of Magnificent Distances, but it might with greater propriety be termed the City of Magnificent Intentions … Spacious avenues, that begin in nothing, and lead nowhere; streets, mile-long, that only want houses, roads, and inhabitants; public buildings that need but a public to be complete; and ornaments of great thoroughfares, which only lack great thoroughfares to ornament, are its leading features.

—Charles Dickens, British author, 1842

economy. In Washington, D.C., more government workers were hired. Factories and farms across the country reopened to produce supplies for the war effort.

After the war, things in the district began to change once again. Many of the white residents living in the district began to move to the surrounding suburbs. They still worked in Washington, D.C., but they lived in homes that were 15 miles (24 km) or more away. At the same time, more and more African Americans were moving up from the South. The result was that, by 1960, the population of Washington, D.C., was 54 percent African American.

The District of Columbia, at that time, had a bigger population than many states. Yet it still had no voice in its own political affairs. In 1960, Congress

Bethesda, a suburb of Washington, D.C., is home to about 60,000 people. Unlike Washington, D.C., it has a very small African-American population.

Dr. Martin Luther King Jr. was a respected leader of the Civil Rights movement. His famous "I Have a Dream" speech was given in Washington, D.C.

Although Congress meets in Washington, D.C., the district's residents are only able to elect one non-voting member to the House of Representatives.

changed this situation slightly, when it approved the Twenty-third Amendment to the US Constitution. This amendment finally gave the residents of Washington, D.C., the right to vote in presidential elections.

The 1960s were a time when black people all over the country were demanding to be treated like all other Americans. Across the country, African Americans were often treated differently from white people. They were not allowed the same rights as white people. For example, special areas were set aside in restaurants for blacks only, and African Americans were forced to ride at the back of city buses and give up their seats to white people. African-American children were forced to go to all-black schools, which were usually not as good as the all-white schools. The civil rights movement had developed to fight these inequalities. The movement had one of its most historic moments in Washington, D.C., on August 28, 1963. More than 200,000 people of many races marched to the steps of the Lincoln Memorial to hear the Reverend Martin Luther King Jr. give his famous "I Have a Dream" speech.

On April 4, 1968, Dr. King was assassinated in Memphis, Tennessee, which was a a great blow to the civil rights movement. In the days that followed, many

Americans were angry, and a number of America's cities, including Washington, D.C., were torn apart by terrible riots. Large sections of Washington, D.C., were destroyed by fire and looting. Nine people were killed, and hundreds more were injured. The areas rebuilt slowly, but some were never the same again. Eventually, African Americans and other minorities were given more equal rights. However, racial equality remained an important issue in many of Washington's neighborhoods.

Beginning in the early 1970s, Washingtonians gained more influence in government. In 1970, they were allowed to elect one nonvoting member to the House of Representatives. This special member could speak in debates and attend hearings, but could not vote for or against laws.

In 1973, Congress finally allowed Washingtonians to elect their own city government. At the time the city, like many other cities across the country, was in serious trouble. Many of the city's residents moved away to the suburbs.

Visitors to Washington, D.C., enjoy learning about US history at sites such as the Lincoln Memorial.

The attack on the Pentagon on September 11, 2001, took more than 180 lives and caused millions of dollars worth of damage.

Poverty was still widespread in the district, and so were drugs and violence. By the 1980s, gang activity had made Washington, D.C., one of America's most dangerous cities, with one of the highest murder rates in the country. Several laws and programs were established to fight these problems, and some success has been made. Washington, D.C., is still rebuilding and trying to improve the lives of its residents.

Washington, D.C., has been affected by world events, as well, and the results have sometimes been very painful. On September 11, 2001, an airplane that was hijacked by terrorists crashed into the Pentagon—the huge military headquarters across the Potomac River. More than 180 people died in the aircraft and on the ground. The district grieved for the losses and slowly rebuilt the Pentagon.

After the attack on the Pentagon, the number of people visiting the city fell. However, in the more than 10 years since, the tourist industry and the city as a whole have recovered. Today, Washington, D.C., is once again becoming the exciting, vibrant city it was meant to be.

Important Dates

★ **From 11,000** BC Paleo-Indians live in the area around the Potomac River.

★ **1600** CE By the time the first European settlers arrive, the region is inhabited by the Piscataway Native Americans.

★ **1632** Henry Fleete builds a trading post on the Potomac River.

★ **1632** The area that now includes the District of Columbia becomes part of the Maryland Colony.

★ **1751** Georgetown—which would eventually become a Washington, D.C., neighborhood—is founded.

★ **1776** The United States of America declares itself independent from Great Britain, starting the Revolutionary War.

★ **1791** With the help of Andrew Ellicott and Benjamin Banneker, Pierre Charles L'Enfant begins to design the capital.

★ **1800** John Adams becomes the first president to live in the still-unfinished White House.

★ **1814** British soldiers occupy Washington during the War of 1812, burning large sections of the city, including the White House.

★ **1865** President Abraham Lincoln is shot at Washington's Ford's Theatre.

★ **1871** Washington, D.C., becomes an official municipal corporation.

★ **1888** The Washington Monument is completed and opened to visitors.

★ **1960** The Twenty-third Amendment gives residents of Washington, D.C., the right to vote in presidential elections.

★ **1963** Martin Luther King Jr. delivers his famous "I Have a Dream" speech during the March on Washington for Jobs and Freedom.

★ **1970** Washington, D.C., is permitted to elect one nonvoting delegate to the House of Representatives.

★ **2001** A plane hijacked by terrorists crashes into the Pentagon, killing more than 180 people.

★ **2011** The Martin Luther King Jr. Memorial is unveiled on the National Mall.

The People

For the first 150 years of its existence, Washington's population grew steadily. In 1800, the nation's new capital had just 14,093 residents. Today more than 600,000 people call the district home. It has the twenty-fourth-largest population of any city in the United States.

These statistics do not give the whole picture, though. At many points over the last sixty years, Washington, D.C., unlike many American cities, has actually been losing people. In 1950, the census showed a population of 802,178. Just ten years later, only 763,956 people lived in the district.

This was a trend that was happening all over the United States, as people moved to the suburbs, seeking better housing and better schools for their children. Few US cities, though, have been hit as hard by this "reverse migration" (people moving out of the city) as Washington, D.C. The population of the city continued to fall. Between 1990 and 2000, the District's population dropped by 5.7 percent. This steady "people drain" caused many problems for the city, such as fewer taxes, which meant less money for schools, police departments, and other services. Things are looking up for Washington, D.C., though. The 2010 census recorded a population growth of nearly 30,000 people!

Beyond the government buildings, national monuments, and historic museums, Washington, D.C., has neighborhoods where many families live.

Washington, D.C., has many good schools for residents of all ages.

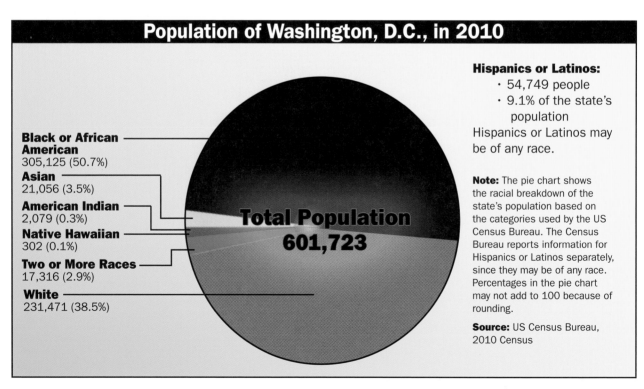

Population of Washington, D.C., in 2010

Black or African American
305,125 (50.7%)

Asian
21,056 (3.5%)

American Indian
2,079 (0.3%)

Native Hawaiian
302 (0.1%)

Two or More Races
17,316 (2.9%)

White
231,471 (38.5%)

**Total Population
601,723**

Hispanics or Latinos:
- 54,749 people
- 9.1% of the state's population

Hispanics or Latinos may be of any race.

Note: The pie chart shows the racial breakdown of the state's population based on the categories used by the US Census Bureau. The Census Bureau reports information for Hispanics or Latinos separately, since they may be of any race. Percentages in the pie chart may not add to 100 because of rounding.

Source: US Census Bureau, 2010 Census

Washington fans enjoy attending sporting events and cheering for the district's sports teams.

Who Are the Washingtonians?

In some ways, Washington, D.C., is very different from most cities in the United States. One key difference is the size and importance of the city's African-American community. In 1960, Washington, D.C., became the first city in the United States to have a majority black population. Today African Americans make up a little more than 50 percent of the city's population. This is very different from the United States as a whole, which is 77.9 percent white and just 13.1 percent black.

Washington's black community has a long, proud history. Many of the most distinguished African Americans throughout history have lived in Washington, D.C. These people include great writers such as Langston Hughes, musicians like Duke Ellington, civil rights leaders including Frederick Douglass, as well as Benjamin Oliver Davis, the first African American to become a general in the US Army. Washington's black community is very proud of its

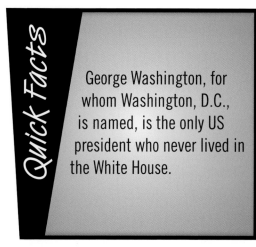

Quick Facts

George Washington, for whom Washington, D.C., is named, is the only US president who never lived in the White House.

historic contribution to the city's history and culture. One of the parts of the Smithsonian Institution, the Anacostia Museum, is dedicated to celebrating African-American history and culture.

The story of Washington, D.C., is not just about black and white, however. The city also has a large Spanish-speaking, or Hispanic, community, mostly centered in the Adams-Morgan neighborhood in Northwest D.C. Hispanics make up about 10 percent of the city's population today. Many of the members of Washington's Hispanic community are recent immigrants from Central America, especially the nation of El Salvador.

There is also a small but vibrant Asian-American community in Washington, D.C. This community is focused around Chinatown, in the Northwest section of the district. It represents slightly less than 4 percent of the city's population. Hundreds of thousands more Asian-Americans live in the suburbs across the Potomac River. Just because the neighborhood is called Chinatown does not mean that only Chinese-Americans live and work there. The city's Asian

Asian-American families in D.C. often come from a variety of Asian nations.

Many Washington families live in elegant houses in D.C.'s neighborhoods.

population comes from many other places, too, including Vietnam, Japan, and other countries in Southeast Asia.

The greater Washington area is one of the country's most important destinations for immigrants. During the 1990s, almost 250,000 people from other countries came to live in the area. Only about 13 percent of them chose to live in the district itself. Most immigrants moved to the suburbs. The largest concentration of immigrants in the district is in the Adams-Morgan neighborhood, where almost 25 percent of all residents were born outside the United States. Immigrants from all over the world make the Adams-Morgan neighborhood one of Washington's most colorful and interesting communities. People from as far away as Ethiopia and Peru have opened shops and restaurants in the area. Adams-Morgan's main street, Columbia Road, offers some of the best ethnic food in the city.

Washington, D.C., sometimes seems like the crossroads of the world. Take a walk along the Mall—or down Massachusetts Avenue or near Dupont Circle—and you may hear a dozen different languages being spoken. This is because Washington, D.C., has a very large number of foreign-born people.

Famous Washingtonians

Duke Ellington: Musician

Many people consider Edward Kennedy "Duke" Ellington one of the most important musicians in American history. Hundreds of Ellington's compositions are still played today. He was born in 1899, in Washington's Shaw District. Ellington went to New York City in the 1920s with his first band, the Washingtonians, and became famous playing at the legendary Cotton Club in Harlem. The Duke Ellington Orchestra toured constantly, appearing in nightclubs and concert halls all over the world, until the Duke's death in 1974.

J. Edgar Hoover: Law Enforcement Official

John Edgar Hoover was born in D.C. in 1895. In 1924, he became the director of the federal government's Bureau of Investigation—later renamed the Federal Bureau of Investigation (FBI)—a position he held until his death in 1972. He first became famous for tracking down gangsters and bank robbers. Hoover was criticized for abusing his power, but even his enemies gave him credit for making the FBI one of the most modern and effective police forces in the world.

Cory Booker: Politician

Cory Booker is the current mayor of Newark, New Jersey. Born in Washington, D.C., in 1969, Booker attended Stanford University and Yale Law School. He is known for his public service and his strong commitment to the people of New Jersey.

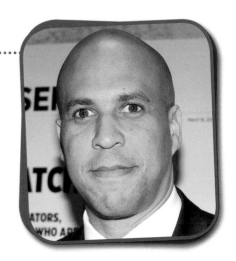

John Philip Sousa: Musician

This famous bandleader and composer, known as the March King, was born in Washington, D.C., in 1854. Sousa led the US Marine band from 1880 to 1892. He then formed his own orchestra, which gave concerts all over the world. Sousa wrote many patriotic compositions that are still performed by marching bands, including "Semper Fidelis," the official march of the US Marines. He died in 1932, after conducting a performance of his most famous composition, "The Stars and Stripes Forever."

Bill Nye: Scientist and Educator

Scientist Bill Nye was born in 1955. His father's family had lived in Washington, D.C., for many generations, and his mother had worked as a code breaker during World War II. Nye is often called "Bill Nye the Science Guy," and he has appeared on many television shows and written several books. He is also still active in the field of science and worked on the development of a sundial as part of the Mars Exploration Rover missions.

Connie Chung: Reporter

Connie Chung was the first Asian American—and only the second woman—to host a nightly network television news program in the United States. The daughter of a diplomat from Taiwan, she was born in Washington, D.C., in 1946 and raised there and in the Maryland suburbs. After studying journalism at the University of Maryland, she went to work as a secretary at a Washington television station. In the almost four decades since then, she has worked for all the major networks, including ABC, CBS, NBC, and CNN.

Many are immigrants, but thousands more are temporary visitors. They work for their countries' embassies or for international organizations with offices in Washington, D.C. Still others are students at Washington's colleges and universities. Many of these people will return to their own countries someday, but some will also make Washington, D.C., their permanent home.

Things to See and Do in Washington

Wherever they come from, Washingtonians love to take advantage of the pleasures the city has to offer. These include cultural activities, ranging from opera and ballet at the Kennedy Center to jazz and blues at the famous Blues Alley club in Georgetown. Many of the district's fine museums attract both residents and visitors.

Washingtonians love to enjoy the outdoors, especially during warm weather. A warm summer day might find Washington's residents rowing a rented boat on the Tidal Basin, shooting hoops on an outdoor basketball court, or enjoying a brass-band concert on the Mall. Residents and visitors love to stroll through

The National Children's Museum, which opened in a new facility in 2012, lets Washington's young residents and visitors learn through play.

Washington, D.C., has many monuments and memorials—such as the Vietnam Veterans Memorial—that honor the brave men and women who have defended the country.

Rock Creek Park, which has large areas that feel almost like wilderness regions. Another favorite outdoor spot is the historic Chesapeake & Ohio Canal National Historic Park. This is a nineteenth-century canal along which people can walk or ride bicycles. They can even ride on barges pulled by mules, just like in the old days. Another great outdoor spot is the Smithsonian National Zoological Park, one of the country's best zoos. It is home to more than 2,000 animals. The zoo's most famous residents are the giant pandas from China.

Some people say the only thing Washingtonians love more than politics is sports. One of the most popular sports in the city is basketball, whether it is played in a schoolyard or by the beloved Georgetown University team. Washington, D.C., has professional basketball, football, and hockey teams. Washingtonians were overjoyed in 2005 when a new team, the Nationals, brought major-league baseball to the city for the first time in more than thirty years.

With its diverse population and interesting sites and events—from museums and festivals to the countless outdoor activities—Washington, D.C., has a lot to offer everyone.

MAKING A SUMMER WREATH

In the early 1800s, stately homes were built for members of Congress and other government officials living in Washington, D.C. Many of these fine homes of brick and wood still exist at the nation's capital. One of the most popular decorations for the front doors of these houses were wreaths—one for winter and one for summer. Follow these instructions to make your own summer wreath.

WHAT YOU NEED:

Dried flowers
Bundle of dry reeds (available at craft stores and many flower shops)
Large container of water

Paper towels
Twine
Scissors
Ribbon

FOR THE DRIED FLOWERS:

You can either dry your own flowers or buy dried flowers from a craft store or flower shop. To dry your own, buy or pick fresh flowers and herbs, such as daisies, rosemary, marigolds, sage, or violets. Tie these with twine in two or three bunches. Hang them upside down in a dark closet or attic for four to six weeks.

TO MAKE THE WREATH:

Place the reeds in a large container of water and allow them to soak for about 20 to 30 minutes until they are soft. Dry them with the paper towel.

Bend and shape the reeds into a circle, overlapping the ends. Use the twine to tie the reeds together at every 4 or 5 inches (10–12.7 cm). You may need a friend or an adult to help you hold the reeds together to be tied.

Once the reeds are securely tied, set them aside and let your wreath dry.

Add the dried flowers to the wreath by gently pushing the flower stems into the reeds. Use bits of twine or ribbon to hold the flowers in place. (You can even use a little bit of glue.) For an extra decoration, make a bow out of the ribbon and fasten it to the bottom of the wreath.

Hang your wreath where your friends and family can admire it or give it as pretty gift!

Calendar of Events

★ **Chinese New Year Parade**

During the Chinese New Year, in January or February, the crowded streets of Chinatown come alive with lion and dragon dancers, drummers, and exploding firecrackers.

★ **Cherry Blossom Festival**

This annual springtime event happens in March or April, when delicate pink and white flowers begin to appear on the Japanese cherry trees in West Potomac. The festival celebrates the close ties between the American and Japanese people, with traditional Japanese music and arts and a huge parade.

★ **Blossom Kite Festival**

Every April, the skies around the Washington Monument fill with kites of every possible shape, size, and color. Children of all ages take kite-making classes and compete for prizes. Every year, the high point of the festival is the Rokkaku Battle, a battle among Japanese-style fighting kites.

★ **White House Easter Egg Roll**

Children have been rolling brightly colored Easter eggs across the White House lawn since 1878 when President Rutherford B. Hayes began the tradition. This favorite Washington event, which includes other games and entertainment, happens every year on Easter Monday.

★ **Smithsonian Folklife Festival**

This exciting event, held in June and July, showcases traditional arts and cultures. As you walk down the National Mall, you might hear a bluegrass band from Kentucky, see multicultural crafts being made, or taste some of the best food in the world.

★ D.C. Caribbean Carnival

Every June, the members of Washington's West Indian community throw the best street party in the city. There is great music, including reggae from Jamaica and steel drums from Trinidad, and a huge parade of spectacular floats and costumes.

★ National Independence Day Celebration

This is probably the biggest Fourth of July festival in the country. Washington, D.C., celebrates America's birthday in grand style, with a parade along Constitution Avenue, a concert on the Capitol steps, and a huge display of fireworks at the Washington Monument.

★ Arlington Cemetery Memorial Day Ceremony

Each Memorial Day, Washington residents and visitors honor the fallen soldiers buried in Arlington National Cemetery. Wreaths are placed at the grave of John F. Kennedy and the Tomb of the Unknown Soldier, and the president often gives a speech at the Memorial Amphitheatre.

★ National Christmas Tree Lighting

This ceremony has been a holiday tradition since 1923. Every year, thousands of people are delighted when a Christmas tree is lit up in the Ellipse, a park near the White House. The event includes a performance from a military band and a holiday message from the president.

How the Government Works

Washington, D.C., has a system of government that is unlike any other place in the United States. The district is the home of the federal government—as well as home to many of the most powerful people in the country—but it also has its own government. The district's government, however, does not function like the government of other cities or states. This is—at least partly—the way the nation's founders wanted it. They feared that the people of Washington, D.C., would be able to control the federal government if the city had too much power. In the process, though, they also limited the power Washingtonians have over their own city's affairs.

For almost a century, Washington had no municipal, or city, government at all. Between 1874 and 1973, the District of Columbia was managed by a congressional committee. This committee—which was appointed, not elected—usually neglected the city. Washington seldom received enough money to build modern schools and hospitals or to keep its roads and bridges in good condition.

Even after the district regained the right to elect its own municipal government, it still lacked some of the basic powers that almost every other city in the United States has. The most important is the ability to raise money.

A statue of Abraham Lincoln stands in front of the Washington, D.C., Superior Courthouse.

Fireworks light up the sky during one of Washington's Fourth of July celebrations.

Most cities pay for the things they need through taxes. The people who live or work in a city pay many taxes on their earnings or on the property they own. The taxes are used to pay for things the district needs. Washington's ability to make people pay taxes, though, is very limited. In most cities, property taxes are the most important source of government funds. In Washington, nearly 60 percent of all property cannot be taxed. This is because it belongs either to the federal government or to foreign countries.

Another problem is that many of the people who work in the district are commuters who live elsewhere. In other large cities where people live in suburbs and commute into the city—such as in New York City—the state makes commuters pay a portion of their income in taxes to the city where they earn their living. Federal law does not allow Washington to do this, which puts a greater burden on the people who do live and pay taxes in Washington, D.C. Property taxes and income tax are much higher in the district than in the surrounding suburbs. This is one of the main reasons so many people choose to live in Virginia or Maryland and commute to their jobs in Washington.

Branches of Government

EXECUTIVE ★ ★ ★ ★ ★ ★ ★ ★
This branch of government is responsible for the day-to-day management of the city. It is headed by the mayor, who is elected to a four-year term by all the voters of the city. A mayor can serve an unlimited number of terms if he or she is re-elected. The mayor appoints people to run the police and fire departments, the school system, and other parts of the city government.

LEGISLATIVE ★ ★ ★ ★ ★ ★ ★ ★
The Council of the District of Columbia votes on proposals for things that the city might choose to do, such as raising property taxes or building new schools. There are thirteen members of the Council. One is elected by the voters in each of the city's eight electoral districts, and five more are elected by all of the city's voters.

JUDICIAL ★ ★ ★ ★ ★ ★ ★ ★
Washington's judicial, or court, system has two levels: the Superior Court and the Court of Appeals. The Superior Court, which has one chief judge, 61 associate judges, and 24 magistrate judges, handles most criminal and civil cases. These range from trials for crimes such as murder and drug trafficking to tax disputes. The Court of Appeals, with one chief judge and eight associate judges, has the power to review any decision made by the lower court. All of Washington, D.C.'s judges are appointed by the president for 15-year terms. There are no limits on the number of terms a judge can serve.

Washington, D.C., also has very limited control over how it can spend the money it raises. In 1995, after the city found itself deep in debt and unable to pay many of its bills, Congress created a control board to oversee Washington's financial decisions. This board, whose members are appointed rather than elected, must give its approval before the city can spend money on new projects.

RECIPE FOR WHITE HOUSE SUGAR COOKIES

It is said that residents of the White House enjoy these delicious sugar cookies. Follow these instructions to make your own tasty treats.

WHAT YOU NEED:

2/3 cup sugar

1/2 cup butter or margarine

2 eggs

1 teaspoon vanilla extract

2 cups all-purpose flour

1 teaspoon salt

2 teaspoons baking powder

Combine the sugar and butter, and beat them until they are light and fluffy. (If you have an electric mixer, ask an adult to help you use it to beat the sugar and butter.) Stir in the eggs and vanilla.

In a separate bowl, combine the flour, salt, and baking powder. Add this mixture to the sugar, butter, vanilla, and eggs. Mix everything together to make a dough.

Wrap the dough in plastic wrap and place it in the refrigerator for at least three hours. (You can even let the dough sit in the fridge overnight.)

Using a rolling pin and a surface lightly covered with flour, roll out the chilled dough until it is even and about 0.25 inch (0.6 cm) thick. Use a knife to cut out shapes, or use cookie cutters to cut out the shapes you like.

Have an adult preheat the oven to 350°F (177°C). Place the cookies on a baking tray. Bake the cookies for ten to twelve minutes or until they are a light brown. You might want to have an adult turn the tray around after about five minutes so the cookies bake evenly. Remove the tray from the oven. Be careful, it will be hot! Let the cookies cool completely before enjoying them.

How You Can Make a Difference

If you live in Washington, D.C., the federal government is practically next door. You can tour the White House and the Capitol, sit in on congressional hearings, and see almost every part of your federal government in action. Even though Washingtonians do not have a direct say in how the federal government is run, they can still make their voices heard. You also have a say in your municipal government.

The best way to begin is by learning as much as you can about the important issues facing the district. Washington's daily newspapers, radio and television stations, and other media outlets offer in-depth coverage of the city's affairs. The Internet is also a very good source of information about politics in the district. Once you have learned everything you can about the issues, contact your federal and municipal representatives by telephone, mail, or e-mail, and let them know what you think. You can make a difference!

Contacting Lawmakers

★ ★ ★ ★ ★ ★ ★ ★ ★ ★ ★ ★

If you are interested in contacting members of the Council of the District of Columbia, go to:

http://www.dccouncil.washington. dc.us/

You can find out more about members of the Council and legislative business.

These kids are campaigning for a candidate in the 2012 presidential election. After all, the new president will be their neighbor!

Making a Living

People who live in Washington, D.C., sometimes call it a "company town." A company town is a place that centers around a single industry. The most important business in Washington, D.C., is the United States government.

About 733,000 people work in the District of Columbia. About one-third of them have government jobs. The US government was the reason Washington, D.C., was created, and it is still the most important element of life in the city. The people who work for the government do an amazing variety of jobs, from sending out tax refunds at the Internal Revenue Service to examining fingerprint evidence at the FBI crime laboratory. You can actually see some government employees at work by taking tours of government buildings. One of the more interesting tours is the one through the Bureau of Engraving and Printing in the Treasury Building, where dollar bills are printed at a rate of 8,000 sheets per minute. The Library of Congress is another good place to visit. This is the largest library in the world, with more than 35 million books and other printed materials.

Government jobs and tourism are the key moneymakers for the district.

Washington's Industries and Workers (May 2013)

Industry	Number of People Working in That Industry	Percentage of Labor Force Working in That Industry
Mining, Logging, and Construction	13,300	1.8%
Manufacturing	900	0.1%
Trade, Transportation, and Utilities	27,100	3.7%
Information	16,400	2.2%
Financial Activities	28,700	3.9%
Professional & Business Services	156,700	21%
Education & Health Services	117,100	16%
Leisure & Hospitality	68,100	9.2%
Other Services	68,300	9.3%
Government	237,200	32.3%
Totals	**733,800**	**99.5%**

Notes: The number of jobs exceeds the population of the district because of the large amounts of people who work in Washington, D.C., but live in its suburbs.

Source: U.S. Bureau of Labor Statistics

These stacks of $5 bills have been printed and counted at the Bureau of Engraving and Printing. The bureau introduced a redesigned $100 bill in 2013.

Anyone who performs a service, rather than making a product, is a service worker. People who work for the government are part of the service industry. Service workers also include doctors, lawyers, teachers, and postal workers. Maintenance workers who provide services that help maintain the district and its site are also service workers.

Many people in Washington, D.C., work for the tourism industry. An estimated 19 million visitors come to Washington, D.C., every year, either as tourists or on business. Visitors to the district take tours of government buildings, admire the monuments and statues in the city's parks, visit the museums, and attend musical performances.

Dedicated workers help to repair and maintain the district's many landmarks.

The arts are an important part of the district. Washington, D.C., draws art lovers from all over the world. The National Gallery of Art and the Hirshhorn Museum and Sculpture Garden have paintings and sculptures from every period and every style. There is no shortage of performing arts, either. The Kennedy Center offers performances by symphony orchestras, opera and ballet companies, and jazz musicians. Washington, D.C., has a lively theater scene, too.

The tourism industry provides jobs for many Washingtonians, such as hotel desk clerks, waiters, travel agents, park rangers, and museum guides. Without them, Washington's attractions could not function.

Transportation

An outstanding transportation network carries travelers to, from, and around Washington, D.C. The city has one of the world's best subway systems, and the second-busiest in the United States. The Metro carries more than 800,000 riders on a typical day. It connects Washington, D.C., with the suburbs where many of the city's workers live.

Interstate highways, including the famous Beltway, carry a huge number of cars and trucks. The greater Washington area's three international airports, the Ronald Reagan Washington National, Dulles International, and Baltimore–Washington International, together handle more than 50 million passengers a year.

Washington's many monuments and memorials, such as the Jefferson Memorial, are popular tourist attractions.

Products & Resources

Museums

The district is home to dozens of museums. These attractions highlight such things as arts, history, dinosaurs, and spacecraft. The Smithsonian Institution has multiple museums and research centers, which offer a great deal for visitors and residents of all ages. With nine million visitors a year, the National Air and Space Museum is one of the most popular museums in Washington, D.C.

Education

Washington has many colleges and universities. Well-known D.C. schools include Howard University, Georgetown, George Washington University, and American University. Thousands of students attend schools in the district, bringing more than $200 million a year into the local economy.

Communications and Media

D.C. is one of the world's great communications centers. Many important newspapers and magazines are published in the district. Most of the world's great newspapers have offices in Washington. All these media outlets rely on a highly advanced communications system that uses satellites and the Internet to keep them in contact with the entire world. In recent years, the D.C. area has become a leader in "new media," with major Internet service providers located around the city.

Currency

Washington's Bureau of Engraving and Printing develops and prints billions of dollars every year, to be delivered to the Federal Reserve System. The US Mint, which manufactures and distributes the country's coins, is also headquartered in Washington, D.C.

Parks

Washington, D.C., is home to many beautiful parks and green spaces. The district contains twenty-three national parks that attract more than 34 million visitors each year. The largest D.C. park, called Rock Creek Park, was established in 1890 and covers an area of 2,820 acres (1,141 ha).

Library of Congress

Established by President John Adams in 1800, the Library of Congress is the national library of the United States and is one of the largest libraries in the world. Today the library contains more than 838 miles (1,349 km) of shelves filled with books, maps, photographs, films, and other materials. These materials cannot be checked out by the general public, but the library does offer visitor tours of the historic building and the chance to view special exhibitions from the vast collection.

Washington, D.C., is known for its efficient Metro system.

Manufacturing and Construction

Washington, D.C., has a small manufacturing industry. Most of the district's manufacturing workers are employed in the printing and publishing industry. They produce newspapers and other publications, as well as printed materials for various parts of the government. Construction is another important segment of the Washington, D.C., workforce. Sometimes it seems as if parts of the city are always being improved or rebuilt. In a typical year, thousands of construction workers may be involved in construction projects around the city.

Many high-tech companies have their headquarters in the Washington area, partly because they need to be close to government agencies that buy their products. Many of these companies, which include software developers and Internet service providers, have chosen to locate in the suburbs. However, in the past few years, there have been signs of high-tech companies moving into the city itself. This is good news for Washington and for its workers.

Looking to the Future

Washington's economy has generally been strong, with the federal government as a steady source of employment. However, in the last few years, Washington, D.C., has had one of the nation's highest unemployment rates, with more than 8 percent of the district's residents unemployed. The nation's capital has a large number of wealthy people, but it also has a very large number of poor people. Government programs and initiatives to improve the district's economy have helped to improve the inequalities, though there is still work to do. Washington's challenge, in the years to come, will be to make sure that all its residents share in the wealth and power that make it one of the world's greatest places.

Washington's monuments and memorials are open 24 hours a day and free to the public so they can be enjoyed by all residents and visitors.

Official Flag & Seal

The official flag of Washington, D.C., is based on George Washington's family coat of arms. It has three red stars and broad red stripes against a white background. The design was chosen by a congressional commission in 1938.

The Washington, D.C., seal shows a blindfolded woman—representing justice—laying a wreath at a statue of George Washington. A bald eagle is at her feet, and the Sun is rising in the background. At the bottom are the words "Justitia Omnibus," which means "justice for all." Also at the bottom of the seal are the numbers 1871, the year the seal was adopted.

Washington, D.C. Map

Rock Creek Park

Military Rd.

29

Tenleytown 410 ft.

Dalecarlia Reservoir

Wisconsin Ave.

Connecticut Ave.

Rock River

16th Street

Georgia Ave.

New Hampshire Ave.

N. Capitol St.

South Dakota Ave.

MacArthur Blvd.

Washington Cathedral

Naval Observatory

Massachusetts Ave.

National Zoological Park

Michigan Ave.

13th Street

McMillan Reservoir

Rhode Island Ave.

1

New York Ave.

Bladensburg Rd.

50

National Arboretum

Kenilworth Aquatic Gardens

Anacostia River Park

Mary McLeod Bethune Council House National Historic Site

Benning Rd.

Theodore Roosevelt Island Memorial

White House

Constitution Ave.

Smithsonian Institute

U.S. Capitol

NATIONAL MALL

E. Capital St.

Lincoln Memorial

Vietnam Veteran's Memorial Wall

Washington Monument

Independence Ave.

395

Anacostia River

Fort Dupont Park

Arlington National Cemetery

Thomas Jefferson Memorial

East Potomac Park

Anacostia Freeway

Frederick Douglass National Historic Site

Pennsylvania Ave.

Potomac River

295

Bolling Air Force Base

Suitland Parkway

Alabama Ave.

miles	
0	3
km	
0	5

	Interstate Highway	▲	Highest Point in the District
	U.S. Highway		National Monument
	State Highway	☆	Historic Site

MORE ABOUT WASHINGTON, D.C.

BOOKS

Edwards, Roberta. *Who Was George Washington?* New York: Grosset & Dunlap, 2009.

Harper, Leslie. *How Do Laws Get Passed?* Civics Q&A. New York: PowerKids Press, 2013.

Ogintz, Eileen. *The Kid's Guide to Washington, D.C.* Kid's Guides. Guilford, CT: GPP Travel, 2013.

Sasek, Miroslav. *This Is Washington, D.C.* New York: Universal, 2011.

WEBSITES

Kids in the House
http://kids.clerk.house.gov/young-learners/lesson.html?intID=29

Smithsonian Institution
http://www.si.edu/

Virtual Tour of Washington, D.C.
http://ahp.gatech.edu/dc_map.html

The White House
 http://www.whitehouse.gov/

Terry Allan Hicks has written several books about the United States, including books on American history and US symbols. He lives in Connecticut with his wife, Nancy, and their children, Jamie, Jack, and Andrew.

★ INDEX ★

NANTUCKET

NANTUCKET

Photographs by David Plowden
Text by Patricia Coffin

A Studio Book
THE VIKING PRESS
NEW YORK

Published in Association with
NANTUCKET HISTORICAL TRUST,
NANTUCKET, MASSACHUSETTS

ACKNOWLEDGMENTS

The author and photographer wish to thank the following for their
helpful advice and assistance in preparing this book: David Carson
of the Nantucket Historical Trust and the Nantucket Conservation Foundation; Elsa Prediger of the Natural Science Center
of the Maria Mitchell Association; Professor Ervin H. Zube,
Department of Landscape Architecture, University of Massachusetts; Edouard Stackpole, editor of the Nantucket *Inquirer
and Mirror;* Sydney Coffin; Charles F. Sayle; Clinton and Edith
Andrews; Professor J. Gordon Ogden of Dalhousie University,
Nova Scotia; Roy E. Larsen, Vice Chairman of the Board,
Time, Inc., and Chairman of the Nantucket Conservation Foundation.

CONTENTS

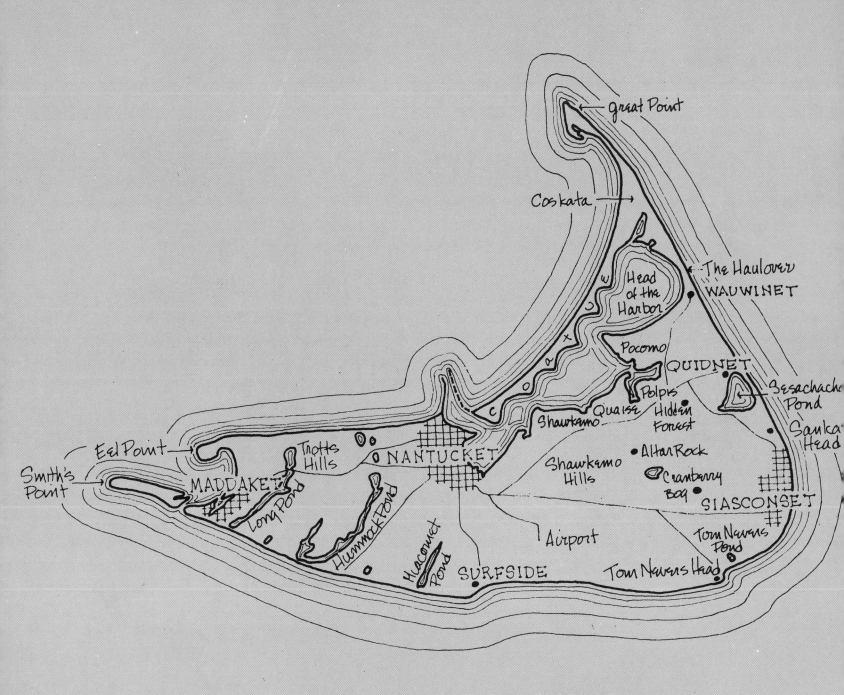

FOREWORD

One of the foremost objectives of the Nantucket Historical Trust is to add to the body of knowledge concerning this island. Because Nantucket is unique historically, architecturally, and ecologically, the work of the Trust, which embraces all these aspects, is of particular interest to scholars of Americana. It is also of deep concern to everyone who envisions the remarriage of man and his environment.

This book, the fourth to be sponsored by the Trust, focuses on the natural surroundings of Nantucket Island, on its geological heritage, its vegetation, its animal life, and, most dramatically, on the changes each season brings to the landscape. The photographs by David Plowden were taken over the span of one year when he visited the island during the winter, in the spring and summer, and finally in the fall. Known for his creative interpretations of the American scene, Plowden worked with the cooperation of a naturalist and of a poet. The text, by Patricia Coffin, is filled with facts that have "flowered into truths."* As she indicates, Nantucket is a subject of fascination to botanists, for the abundance and variety of its vegetation, and to geologists, for its natural formation reflecting the last Ice Age. But for us, the mystique of Nantucket is summed up in one phrase—"the scale is small, the drama is not."

Preservation, another major purpose to which the Trust is dedicated, may sound less exciting to some than innovation. Yet every day we are realizing more and more that the conservation of man's earthly environment may be more important to his future than his explorations of the moon. For: "What is any man's discourse to us if we are not sensible of something in it as steady and cheery as the creak of crickets?"* In this book we hope you will hear "the creak of crickets."

Trustees of the
Nantucket Historical Trust

Henry B. Coleman   George W. Jones   Mary Ann Beinecke
Walter Beinecke, Jr.   K. Dun Gifford

* From "Natural History of Massachusetts" (1842) in Henry D. Thoreau's *Excursions*.

INTRODUCTION

The wind and the sea created Nantucket. They molded her history. They shaped and reshaped her shores. They disciplined her contours and they rewarded her with riches from around the world. Her ancestors are the ten-thousand-years-ago glaciers of the last Ice Age.

In her prime she was queen of a heroic era which ended when the last great Nantucket whaling ship, *The Oak*, sailed out of her harbor in 1869. Her fortunes in sperm oil had collapsed. But Nantucket's true wealth was of another kind. It lay in the gentle beauty of her natural surroundings. And some of the treasures that she retained from overseas included broom from Scotland, ivy from England, the omnipresent salt-spray or rugosa rose whose origins are Japanese, and "patches of . . . true purple Scotch heather . . . a little shy . . . not everyone . . . is invited to its pleasaunce" (Jane B. Austin, 1893). The sea and the wind gave birth to Nantucket, and around the turn of the seventieth century—give or take a thousand years—they will reclaim her.

This heritage has produced an island that is unique. The quality of the landscape, of the historic architecture, and especially of the vegetation and the wildlife is as rare as it is unobtrusive. Nantucket is to be weighed on a jeweler's scale. A fragile, sandy mound—six miles by fourteen and shaped like a blunted harpoon—it surfaces from the Atlantic thirty miles off bedrock-bound New England. It is warmed by the Gulf Stream which passes some two hundred miles south of Nantucket on its way due northeast to Ireland. Nantucket is besieged by hurricanes from the tropics and storms from the northeast that get a three-hundred-mile running start across the water from Nova Scotia. Her trees are warped by the wind (southwest prevailing), and the "parent material" of her soil is sand. Moist summer fogs roll in from the ocean, muffling her moors in mystery, while the sun continues to shine on the mainland. Despite and more probably because of these factors Nantucket has more varied vegetation than any other area of the same size in America. It is a meeting ground for northern and southern plants—plants that may have originated a hundred centuries ago, such as ground-hugging bearberry, golden heather with its tiny yellow flowers—and plants that came during the tropical spell a mere thousand years ago, including holly, sour gum, and golden aster. Prickly pear cactus blooms in July on Coatue, that elegantly scalloped peninsula enclosing Nantucket Harbor. Called the "Coatue cactus," it grows a clamshell's throw from wintergreen and reindeer moss.

For sheer luxuriance many Nantucket flowers and shrubs are unequaled. Shadblow is one. For two or three days at the end of April this tree-sized bush veils the moors with a pinkish-white mist like a fall of March snow. One variety singular to the island has a bronze leaf and is dignified with the name *Amelanchier Nantucketensis*. Nowhere else does broom crowberry, also called mattress grass, grow in such large patches. It is low, springy to walk on, and sere. The "Nantucket lily," actually the wood lily protected by the State of Massachusetts, erupts in hundreds of low, bright orange flames all over the moors about the middle of August. Only an off-islander would pick one, for once picked they don't grow again. Cockspur thorn, a dramatically tall hawthorn which flourishes in a glen off the road to Quidnet, is found only on Nantucket, says botanist E. P. Bicknell. Thistles grow to a size I've seen flourishing in the south of France, and in May the bird-foot violets near Altar Rock are like blue sheets of fallen sky. The cattail that does best in the brackish waters around the edges of Nantucket's salt marshes is the narrow-leafed, not the common variety. It has crossbred, as often happens on the island, and there are now slim, medium, and fat cattails in the bogs.

There are three stories to tell about Nantucket. One concerns her modern economy in which people and tourism play the leading roles. As one wit remarked: "Summer people and some are not." Another relates to her extraordinary whaling history, at the height of which Nantucket was a curiously sophisticated Quaker community with two and a half times her present population. And then there is the tale that tells of the eternities: the tides and the currents, the nesting grounds of tern and gull, the moors and hidden forests. This is the one that concerns us here. "Far from the shadow of the Three Bricks . . . moss grows thick and cushions the step . . . here is the essence of the island. This is the Nantucket that endures. Has endured. Must—" says Margaret Yates, speaking for the Nantucket Conservation Foundation which is part of today's story, too. The plans to keep at least one-tenth of the island in its original wild state and to preserve the inherited character of its architecture combine to form a truly creative approach to the complexities of modern ecology. This is possible because Nantucket, "way offshore, more lonely than the Eddystone Light . . .," is self-contained, a perfect laboratory for a delicate experiment in balancing beauty and tradition with "progress."

Geologists assert that Nantucket has "the most remarkable terminal moraine anywhere in the world." The last glaciers, feeling the rise in temperature from the Gulf Stream when they hit the New York area, started to melt, releasing vast masses of ice, earth, and stone. As these tons of debris-loaded ice stumbled east over the hills of what was then a vast coastal plain, they dumped their load. The melt water raised the sea level and what land was not drowned became Nantucket, Martha's Vineyard, and Cape Cod. "The buried backbones of the cape and islands," says geologist Barbara Blau Chamberlain, "are the old coastal plain hills." The tops of these hills loop across the center of Nantucket, reappear on Tuckernuck and again on Chappaquiddick next to the Vineyard. They are the clearly visible edge of the moraine. South of this ancient demarcation on Nantucket, the outwash plain fans out. It is dented north to south with "a multiplicity of glacial dumbrils," to quote R. A. Douglas-Lithgow, which were caused by the final melting. A ride to Altar Rock will demonstrate this. It is a "Nantucket roller coaster ride" as opposed to a "Nantucket sleigh ride"—being hauled through the sea by a harpooned whale.

Two *un*common happenings had an enormous influence on the natural character of the island. These were caused by the sheep "commons" and their owners, the first white inhabitants. By the early nineteenth century some seventeen thousand sheep were roaming the land which had been declared "common" pasture. For one hundred and fifty years they destroyed the vegetation and trampled the moors. Bearberry cannot take being marched over any more than it can take being driven over.

So the question is moot: which is worse, the jeep of today or the sheep of yore?

Fallen tree trunks embedded in Nantucket's native peat suggest that "wolf" oak and beech of enormous circumference and with vast root systems were growing there when the first settlers landed in 1659. But by 1670 logs were being imported from the mainland and residents were fined for cutting trees on Coatue—evidence that the new arrivals had stripped their own island of wood. The controversy over how heavily wooded Nantucket originally was remains unresolved, but many believe that with her sandy soil and exposed location she could not have supported tall "ship timber" or "cathedral" forests.

As soon as the sheep were fenced in, the island vegetation began to recover. In fact it flourished. Perhaps the sun-warmed open spaces gentled by frequent enveloping fogs encouraged the growth of bayberry, huckleberry, and shadblow. These form bushy islands in a sea of low-bush blueberry, wild rose, elderberry, and beach plum. They rise from shallows of broom crowberry, bearberry, poverty grass, sweet fern, and dozens of varieties of wild flowers, among the most appealing of which are modest white blossoms called Quaker-ladies. They make their appearance in the spring.

I have been describing the moors which give Nantucket her mystique. They are called "heaths" by botanists because they are oceanic, sandy, and covered with heath plants. But to Nantucketers they seem more akin to the wild moors of Scotland which stretch like the sea to the horizon. There are ten thousand acres of this heath-moorland on the island, unique in this part of the world. The remarkable scale that rules Nantucket is best seen here. To stand on Folger Hill and look in any direction is to feel isolated in a landscape that has no end. No city skyline or mountain range intrudes. The outline of the town in the distance is low, with two church steeples dominating. Few vertical obstructions throw it out of scale.

Even the "street furniture"—fences, houses, benches—are the right size and relationship to each other. The trees do not overwhelm for they have been beaten to their knees by the wind so that some fifty-year-old growths are no higher than twenty feet.

In 1875 Henry Coffin imported from Great Britain thirty thousand Scotch pines and firs and ten thousand larch trees. The late Will Gardner, island historian, believed that the true heather came over with this shipment. Nowadays pitch pine and scrub oak are doing so well that they are beginning to encroach on the moors. They are vegetal predators, as the thick-lipped and thin-lipped oyster drill are predators of the marine variety. However, "the biggest predator I know," said one harbor master, "has two legs and walks."

From the beaches we hear the story of erosion. Slam! Bang! Roar! And hiss! —the ocean has been worrying Nantucket's southeast and western shores for eons and will keep right on until its work is finished. The shoreline along Tom Nevers Head and to the west loses nine acres a year. In 1961 Smith's Point was cut off by Hurricane Esther and has been called Esther Island ever since. Around 1900 the farmers used to drive their cattle at low tide from Smith's Point to Tuckernuck for summer grazing. More than a hundred years before that, two islands existed where shoals now break the water off Madaket. On the other hand, the sand strip below the Sankaty bluffs is widening and the currents around Great Point are building up Coskata Beach and Coatue.

Nantucket has seven good-sized ponds—her "jewels," made of that precious mineral, fresh water. They are rich with perch, pickerel, alewives, and ringed with Virginia creeper, winterberry, and deer tracks. In Long Pond huge snapping turtles deplete the coveys of the haughty mute swan. Largest, Sesachacha Pond, once an inlet, is brackish because it is opened every year to the sea for mosquito control.

The peaty bottoms of former ponds now nourish groves of ancient beech, swamp maple, oak, twisted tupelo, house-high native holly, and sassafras trees in whose branches the wind makes a constant sea-breathing sound. These are the hidden forests out Polpis way, their tops contoured to the land. To be in one is to enter a world beyond. There is deep, rustling quiet. Birds flit through the striated green and gold half light—chickadees, flickers, crested flycatchers who always put a cast-off snakeskin into their nests. In one secret place cardinal flowers bloom in August near a freshwater spring called Eat Fire. They are scarlet exclamation points against the green tapestry of shoulder-high cinnamon fern, meadow rue, viburnum, and jewelweed which soothes the burning itch that poison ivy and stinging nettles give. The treetops are sun-tipped cupolas. Dead leaves rust-color the forest floor. A mammoth old beech is spreading, grandfatherly, with gnarled roots, knuckled like an old man's hand. Its elephantine bark is scarred with initials. Some must date back to 1900 when it was the vogue for young ladies in long skirts, and their beaux, to drive out to the Hidden Forest on Sunday afternoon for a stroll.

It is characteristically odd that no drifts of daffodils, snowdrops, or narcissus materialize in these Nantucket woodlands come spring. Nor do any squirrels, chipmunks, or raccoons inhabit the trees. No foxes hide in the brush, and there are no wildcats, weasels, skunks, porcupines, or muskrats on the island. However, some three hundred white-tailed deer roam the moors. Quail, woodcock, and pheasant thrive in the native cover, and cottontail rabbits are prolific. Enormous jackrabbits leap about the Coskata dunes and Eel Point. In summer Nantucketers ride to hounds after them, having no foxes. By contrast the bird population, resident and/or in transit, seems limitless. Once a paragraph in Sydney Coffin's column "Bird Tracks" read as follows: "September: common loon, piebilled grebe and gannet, black crowned night heron and American egret, Canada goose, mallard, common black duck—osprey, piping plover, ruddy turnstone and woodcock, Wilson's snipe, Hudsonian curlew, solitary sandpiper, eastern and western willets, greater and lesser yellowlegs—"

Some island animals have developed idiosyncrasies due to their isolation. This accounts for the short tail, itty-bitty ears, and dumpy shape of a sub-species of Nantucket house mouse. Muskeget Island, off Tuckernuck, has its mouse, originally a meadow mouse. It now burrows in the dunes and has become a beach vole. The tiny, short-tailed shrew that inhabits Nantucket is unique. But so is the one on the Vineyard, as well as the one on the Cape.

So Nature gives and takes away. Zen student Alan Watts advises us to realize "the inseparable relationship between things . . . and so rediscover the universe." Nantucket and the sea, the sea and the wind and the moors are inseparable. The moor lily, the mussels clamped to the rock, the mole in the meadow are interrelated. Let man rediscover his place in their midst.

WINTER

Winter comes late to Nantucket. Passing waters from the Gulf of Mexico postpone the deep freezes until the new year. Garden flowers decorate Thanksgiving tables, and freshly picked tomatoes are often part of Christmas dinner. As the season advances the scallops firm up. The best cod are caught in the really cold weather. Until the ponds freeze over, they provide plenty of freshwater fish which are in demand as the big commercial saltwater catches are shipped off-island to New Bedford. A winter sport is eeling through a hole cut in the ice off the Madaket pier. "But few people cook eels any more," says a Main Street merchant. "We live differently now. I remember my parents' winter cellar—tubs filled with potatoes, turnips, sun-dried apples, cornmeal. These days it is easier to go to the supermarket than to get poison ivy picking berries. More farms have been sold in the past ten years than in fifty before that."

In midwinter arctic seabirds arrive from the north—geese, ducks, eiders, golden-eyes, mergansers, murres, dovekies, and auks. They seek Nantucket's milder waters. There was a time when brant were so thick on the point at the entrance to Nantucket Harbor that it was named for them. They are rarely seen today, especially around busy Brant Point. Seals swim up Hither Creek after the herring, their heads sticking out of the water like dogs'. Harbor seals winter in Nantucket waters and gray seals live there the year round. Sometimes a herd of thirty is to be seen hauled up on a shoal.

Then in January and February winter settles in. Well into March the storms are wild and bitter. "Years back," recounts artisan-historian Charles F. Sayle, "the fishing schooners iced up so bad that rigging an inch in diameter would be built up to ice over a foot . . . sometimes thirty or forty tons of ice would build up on them. Once in a while a vessel would have to head for the Gulf Stream to melt the great mass off, or go under." A real nor'wester screams in the rigging so that the sailor may not hear the "sudden long booming undertone of surf under the lee bow"—meaning *shoals*.

Twenty-three miles south and east of Sankaty Light lie the Nantucket Shoals, one of the more dangerous stretches of coastline in the United States. Hundreds of ships have been wrecked here within sight of land, even of home. Another wide band of corrugated sea bottom lurks west of Tuckernuck. These are submerged glacial moraines, always changing, so that charts for Nantucket Sound have been revised fifteen times in the past ten years. In no other part of the world where the tides have such a small rise and fall are there such strong currents running far out to sea. Beyond the shoals is the abyss. Here is the edge of the Continental Shelf—a drop of more than a mile in depth.

But the shoals absorb some of the shock from the waves eternally crashing onto

Nantucket's south shore. A mountain of green water forty feet high and five hundred feet long, roaring in with flying mane, exerts 6400 tons of pressure per square foot as it bombards the beach. It carries with it stones, pebbles, sand from down the coast. The sea endlessly tumbles, grinds, polishes its stones into grains of sand. Some grains are long and greenish black, others are paper-thin mica and feldspar. There are shiny grains of quartz, tiny bits of red garnet, round green dots of olivine, and sometimes purple amethyst, tourmaline, beryl, and sapphire. They mix on the beach with the snow crystals.

Winters are not as cold as they used to be. These days Nantucketers do their ice-boating on the ponds instead of the inner harbor, and reminisce about the times when they could haul their dories from Muskeget to Eel Point across the ice. Usually the freeze-up in the harbor is drift ice from the north and west. Prevailing winds jam the big blocks of frozen snow and saltwater between Tuckernuck and Great Point. But some winters Nantucket still gets frozen in and only airplanes can reach her. The ice will extend for two miles off the south shore and across Nantucket Sound toward the Cape. Nantucket Harbor will be frozen solid and so will Madaket. It may take days for the wind and the tides (with the help of a Coast Guard tug) to break the frigid masses. This ties up the scallop fleet, which means a serious loss of winter revenue to the island.

Another crop for which Nantucket is famous is her cranberries. The bog, once the world's largest, lies in marshy fosse valley terrain north of Gibbs Pond. The fruit is a member of the heath family. The Indians knew its nutritional worth, and Nantucket sea captains soon learned that a couple of barrels of cranberries in the hold would curb scurvy during a long voyage.

The face Nantucket shows in winter is in dramatic contrast to her gentle summer mien. Her harbors are wrapped in arctic quiet. Snow fringes her shoreline, and the frozen sands of Coatue are a meager barrier against the bitter chill of the outer beach. The sun is a diamond in the glacial sky. Gulls float by in icy silence, foraging for food. Underneath this blanket of cold the Nantucket landscape lies dormant in expectation of spring. "The temperature falls," editorialized the Nantucket *Inquirer and Mirror* one seven-degree day, "and so we become stoics, learning from nature that winter is a time for waiting and for hoping and for gauging our thoughts. Who will say that the last is not the best." One last thought that winter prompts: we may be living in an interglacial stage and fifty thousand years from now an overwhelming ice sheet could descend on this part of the world again—erasing everything.

Along the south shore

Rose hips and bayberry

Cranberries in the
snow at Gibbs Pond

Pitch pine tree branch

Post - and - rail
fence, Quidnet

Sunrise off Siasconset

Great Point

SPRING

Early spring can be cold as a witch's heart, with frost on the ground and ice crackling in the beach grass. But by late April and May wave upon wave of blooming wild flowers break over the moors. They come in overlapping sequences—first misty shadblow, then the popcorn of beach plum, followed by viburnums, white-flowering chokeberry, and elderberry. Later wild iris and bird-foot violets enrich the landscape with their colors borrowed from the sea: pale to marine blues, deepening into purple.

Those who remark on the absence of spring woodland flowers forget that spring in Nantucket belongs to the moors. True, in the shelter of the woods some anemones appear, also false lily-of-the-valley, sarsaparilla, and colicroot. Warblers (yellow-throat, redstart, and pine), catbirds, and towhees sing in the sun-sequined dusk. Mockingbirds and cardinals join other birds in Nantucket's gardens. Escapees from these gardens are plants originally brought over from Europe for their medicinal qualities. Now growing wild are horehound, catnip, spearmint, and peppermint, also yarrow, boneset, and tansy.

To explore the moors in early June is to see Japanese black pine sending up new candles, daisies thick as stars in an August sky, dark green Scotch broom covered with fat butter-yellow flowers. And growing in with the heath plants: blue-eyed grass, yellow sun roses, wild black cherry bushes, wild geranium, and the white, straw-textured heads of pearly everlasting. "Sticky" azaleas, lavender, pennywort, and the round-flowered buttonbush bloom in the swamps. Beside the roads that run like ribbons over the landscape, bearberry and mattress grass are springy underfoot. In some clumps of pitch pine and scrub oak a last frost line is visible. The trees look green above, and dead below the level where a late frost settled in pockets among the hummocks.

A pair of Canada geese are convoying their fluffy family across a pond in Polpis, and the gulls are nesting on their favorite beaches. Straw trails from under rugosa rose bushes betray where they have laid their eggs—always a clutch of three, large and olive green, mottled with dark gray specks. On Coskata purple beach pea is in flower, and pasture roses have been encouraged to come out by the heat reflected from the sun-baked sand. There are low feathery sea blite and tall seabeach worm-wood, furry golden beach poverty grass and lifeless-looking high tide bush. Spread over the sand at the Haulover on the way to Great Point, a carpet of seabeach sandwort is succulent, thick, and bright green. A horned lark flies up and away, as a least tern takes off, flying low. It is panicked that its little nest will be found on the bare sand between the high tide line and where the beach grass dune begins.

In the crouching shelter of twisted oak trees the bracken grows tall in the Coskata woods and the fiddleheads are ready for spring-salad eating. Neighboring Coatue cedars are low to the ground, wind-flattened, stripped, skeletal, hardly recognizable as a tree that normally stands tall like a blue-black flame. Here with its forty-five-degree haircut, it reroots itself, becomes umbrella-shaped. Mountains, not bushes, of rugosa roses (known also as Japanese sea-tomatoes) are covered with crimson, pale pink, and white blossoms under the soft spring sky. Juniper and rum cherry shrubs are dark green against the silvery beach grass always flowing with the wind. A horseshoe crab plods by, a living fossil whose ancestry goes back four million years. He is preglacial, prehistoric. At the water's edge there are periwinkles, hermit crabs, holes in the sand where soft-shell clams have spit up into the air, and everywhere bird tracks like smocking in the blue satin of the beach.

From the marshy edge of a kettle hole the chorusing of spring peepers reaches a crescendo—a reminder, somehow, of how short this season is. There are also green frogs and pickerel frogs on Nantucket. The kettle hole is a miniature pond ringed with grasses, vines, and wild flowers. It was originally caused by an itinerant block of ice that stayed behind, made a depression, and finally melted into the ground, as opposed to a kame, which is a bump in a hollow where the ice left a lump of debris. In summer these landlocked islets are freckled with tiny asterisks of golden aster.

The exhilaration in the air is the smell of springtime in Nantucket, permeated by the sweet scent of trailing arbutus. Each season has its special fragrance. In summer sweet pepper bush and honeysuckle mingle with the smell of pine. In autumn bayberry and the pungent perfume of wild grapes dominate the moors where the vines cover acres, spill over the weather-silvered sides of post-and-rail fences, climb hawthorn trees, and wrestle with blackberry bushes. In winter the compelling smell of woodsmoke draws a man to his fireside. Some people can smell snow, and many Nantucketers swear that they can smell bluefish when they are swimming beyond the breakers.

When approaching the coast of America more than three hundred years ago, John Winthrop reported "a smell off the shore like the smell of a garden," and near the Narrows, Henry Hudson's crew sniffed grass and flowers, "and very sweet smells came from them." The aroma that came from the profusion of wild flowers on Manhattan Island stopped two Dutch surveyors in their tracks "because we did not know what it was we were meeting!" In spite of the automobile, nature's bouquet is still fresh on Nantucket, an ageless island that miraculously retains some of the innocence of her early days.

Cactus on Coatue

High-bush blueberry flowers near Shimmo

New leaves burst from a grapevine

Broom crowberry

Pink moccasin

Rugosa rose leaves

Beyond the Jetties toward Nantucket Sound

At Cisco

Off Nobadeer

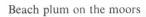
Beach plum on the moors

Low-bush blueberries in a pitch pine forest

Quaker-ladies

Young gulls in beach grass on Coatue

Wind-whipped cedars

Gull's
nest

Herring gull

Canada geese on pond near Quaise

Long Pond

Pond,
vkemo

Rugosa roses near Maxcy's Pond

SUMMER

The summer sun pours down upon the limitless lamé of the Atlantic. The breakers at Cisco gather themselves, curl lazily, and crash to the beach. On the dunes—low, refined like Nantucket herself—the beach grass ripples and flashes in the breeze. It is the first plant to take hold on a dune. Then the wild cranberries, bayberry bushes, beach plum, and wild roses venture over. Just above the tide line sea lavender, seaside spurge, saltwort, and dusty miller (a milky aquamarine) have taken root. Offshore the seabirds wheel and dive and argue with each other—herring gulls and big blackbacks, common terns, black-bellied plovers and sanderlings. Sandpipers twinkle-toe beside the undulating water's edge. The fifty-five miles of gleaming, sandy beaches that outline Nantucket have come into their own.

In the quiescent ocean bluefish and striped bass are running. They came in May, will take off in October. Inshore small shrimp and blue crab go about their business. But lobsters, unlimited in quantity in the 1880s and still plentiful enough for export into the middle 1930s, moved away in the 1950s. Nantucket oysters have never grown large enough to become a commercial success. Mussels and clams make their home at Eel Point and around the Jetties, two long low dikes reaching out from the mouth of Nantucket Harbor. These were built to keep the harbor open after "the bar" had been dredged. This last was a sandbar over which the bigger whaling vessels could not pass, so in the mid-nineteenth century a drydock contraption called "the camels" was constructed to float the big ships over. The whaleship *Constitution* was the first customer.

Above the beaches the sky is limitless, putting the island into perspective: Melville's "ant-hill in the sea," where the clam-diggers on the distant flats seem indeed the size of ants. The sun is a burning glass in the deep blue. Hydrangea bushes stand in inky pools of shade. They are so lush with their fat denim-blue, pink, and mauve balls of blossoms that they look like huge quilted tea-cozies imported from England. The sun comes up with the panache of a painting by Turner and sets into a green mackerel sky that is flecked with a thousand salmon-colored, cornflake-shaped clouds. Evenings the moon grows huge.

Polygala is bursting into tiny magenta blossoms on the moors, pretending to be heather, which is also flowering in rare patches among the pines near Miacomet. Although it has been here more than a hundred years, the Scotch heather is still a struggling off-islander. Buttercups, masses of one-eyed daisies, cat's-ears and yellow goatsbeard, black-eyed Susans and evening primrose spread a golden glow over the hills. Their profusion is breathtaking. Pink sabbatia borders some ponds, and the salt marshes abound with samphire, marsh rosemary, and showy five-petaled rose mallow. The edge of Hummock Pond Road by the cemetery will soon be pale pink with furry rabbit-foot clover.

Behind a hedge on Vestal Street an oval English garden traps the sun. It is a bowl filled with the sweet fragrance of feathery summer lilac bowing to pink, cat-whiskered cleome over banks of patient lucy and alyssum. There are also pinks (with their "pinked" petals) and satellite petunia (purple and white), as well as orange-starred calendula and heliotrope dark as thunder, Johnny-jump-ups and gillyflowers (otherwise known as stock), phlox, snapdragon, and candytuft. All these are swirled around a bee-buzzing bed of thyme. These garden flowers outdo their wild relatives with their extravagance, but remember they have been culti-vated, protected, and cared for.

Meanwhile, song sparrows and yellowthroats sing all summer long. Brown thrashers, chewinks, and kingbirds are everywhere. Over the moors and into the woods, shadowy, silent, sail the red-tailed and sparrow hawks. A short-eared owl beats softly along the grass. Berries are beginning to form—huckleberries, blue-berries, blackberries, beach plum, rose hip, and mealy plum, which is also called bearberry. Starting in mid-August, one after another, they will ripen.

Then, suddenly, fog. From the southeast by the State Forest next to the airport, like ghostly surf it rolls across the island to Dionis Beach, shrouding all with silence, except for the ocean breathing and, high up, somewhere the muffled purr of an aircraft. Moisture drips from the leaves, droplets form on the grass, the plants drink. Small animals walk in safety. A deer crosses the road in the mist. The fog-horn at the end of the Jetties is wailing, wailing.

Late summer is hurricane weather, too. These vicious storms come hurtling up from the Caribbean, and when they hit, the damage is more devastating than that of the bitterest nor'easter. Battered by high seas and ninety-mile-an-hour winds, the island seems to crouch and hold on, to keep from sliding into the sea. In 1938 the ocean broke across Broad Creek causing severe erosion to Cisco and Smith's Point. Hurricane Carol briefly cut Smith's Point off in 1954, and Esther completed the job seven years later. Tropical storms and milder winters are new phenomena that Nantucket shares with the eastern seaboard.

Nantucket's varying vegetation, the subtleties of her summer landscape, her abundant bird population, the wild animals that inhabit her woods and moorlands need a *seeing* eye. The scale is small, the drama is not. Texture of green upon green, plants recognizable by shade, shape, and height can't be caught at a glance. Some of the most colorful flowers are tiny. The ground cover varies from shiny green to sere bluish gray to emerald velvet. To know and to see this, it is necessary to stop and look down, to look up and listen.

Fisherman's shack on Coatue

Cedars

Coatue

Maxcy's Pond

Long Pond

Maxcy's Pond

Field daisies

Lion's-tooth

Field of vetch

Wild arrowwood viburnum

Thistle

Heath plants

Masses of bayberry

Bearberry

Kingbird on a Japanese pine

Short-eared owl over salt marsh. BELOW: Baby gull in poison ivy

Cottontail
at Shimmo

Cinnamon fern   Long beach fern

OVERLEAF: Road over the moors, and a white-tailed deer

Swamp maples in
the Hidden Forest

Eel grass from Madaket Harbor
piled up on Eel Point beach

Horseshoe crab

Quahaug shell and eel grass

Slipper and limpet shells

OVERLEAF: Painted turtle and a scallop shell

Seaweed   Beach poverty grass   Fiddler crab

AUTUMN

A swan flies high over Eel Point looking like a 747 jet—all neck. Below him snow buntings, sparrows, Lapland longspurs—landbirds all—swoop in curlicues of flight. Gulls go sliding down the sky. The blunted, sandy point is an ivory arm set in a sapphire sea under a lapis sky, for it is October. The air is incredibly clear and cool, although the midday sun still warms the sand. Part of Eel Point is a matchless salt marsh, blue-green against the fall-inflamed Dionis moors. It is bordered by Nantucket Sound to the north. To the west it faces Madaket Harbor, ample cradle of baby blues, bass, scallops. This is the sunset end of the island. A "V" of ducks is flying south. Two herons glide low over a golden sheet of shallow water. Great cirrus scarves of rose and orange are flung up into the evening sky from behind low-lying Tuckernuck Island, opposite. Briefly, the sinking sun outdoes the burning samphire in the marsh. And always from across the harbor comes the soft persistent thunder of the sea, fretting the gap between Madaket and truncated Smith's Point.

Tattered ragbags of eel grass have been flung up onto the beach. This is good news, for a cycle is being repeated. Eel grass shelters clams, quahaugs, mussels "as big as bananas," says a resident of Hither Creek. Bay scallops depend on it for food, eat the organic matter from the leaves. When the eel grass "went" in 1931, attacked by a fungus, with it went many fish and mollusks and, in turn, food for diving ducks. For years scallops, the crop by which Nantucket makes her winter living, were scarce. Migrating birds changed their flyways, and in autumn the skies over the marshes were no longer dense with duck and geese. After nearly forty years the eel grass is back and fishing is good again. Old-timers recall the legend in which an Indian sage prophesied: "When the houses of the red man are laid low, the bluefish will return." For some years there had been no bluefish. Then a plague nearly wiped out Nantucket's Indian population in 1764, and after the siege was over and the old chief had died, the bluefish came back.

Islanders get up at four these dark mornings and go duck hunting on Muskeget. They get back in time to open their stores by eight-thirty. The rabbits are a population explosion. Pheasant, woodcock, quail make for the "no hunting" cover near Quidnet and Quaise. The deer bed down in the lee of Hummock Pond. They are descended from the buck who was found swimming offshore in 1922 and mated four years later with the two does imported for him from Michigan by the late Breckinridge Long. Crickets and grasshoppers sing their swan song. Moles, painted turtles, milk, garter, and ribbon snakes, field mice, and shrews take their time preparing for winter.

Blazing garlands of poison ivy, from vivid vermilion to deepest maroon, drape trees, shrubs, fences and run like brush fire along the ground. It's been there all along, a pervading, handsome plant, but in the fall it flames up in all its glory. A species of sumac, the birds like the seeds and they scatter them all over the island. The great cranberry bog is a lake of wine-red fruit. The ocher band that outlines Nantucket is seaside goldenrod. It grows nowhere else in such profusion. A north-west wind hurls itself across the sun-bright water at the Head of the Harbor. It pounces on Wauwinet and moves on to Squam through manes of tawny grass like lion's fur—a thing alive.

The moorland on Tuckernuck is smoldering, aglow. It is a playback to Nan-tucket where bush and tree and vine, ground-cover and the lush late blooming of wild flowers create an iridescence around the cobalt blue of the ponds. The moors are on a rampage of color, a veritable VIBGYOR (spectrum): violet, indigo, blue, green, yellow, orange, and red, plus every mutation thereof. Under shiny dark green leaves the bearberries are Christmas red.

In town the trees have also turned. Here they grow tall, protected by buildings and cared for by man. The plane trees have loosed their leaves onto the cobble-stones. There are three magnificent specimens: one on Washington Street, one at the head of Swain's Wharf, and one in the center of Harbor Square. Their generous trunks and larger branches are liver-spotted with pale yellow and gray. The wine-glass elms that Henry Coffin introduced on either side of Main Street in the 1850s had a setback in the 1930s, many of the diseased ones being cut down. Now they are growing back, complementing the old houses with their grandeur.

The sun's arc is getting lower in the sky. In the intense light everything seems backlit. Soon it will be the shortest day of the year, the smell of wet leaves giving way to the incense of logs burning in hundreds of Nantucket fireplaces. Out over the harbor the seagulls' cry—raucous, wild—is Nantucket's leitmotiv. It speaks of surf smashing on a deserted beach, of rain-soaked wharves and creaking piles, of the northwest wind shifting to northeast, lashing the cowering trees. Then it dies down to the mewling of a child. Yet the mild weather persists. But by mid-December the moors and the shore are left to themselves. Autumn's violet dusk sifts in and settles in the little forest of twisted, low-growing oak trees on Tuckernuck. Birds begin to arrive from the north. Man turns inward, leaving the fields and the woods and all that inhabit them in blessed solitude. Slaughter of sparrow by hawk continues, murder of mouse by owl. But that is nature's balancing act and not to be questioned. It is for man to learn to relate to his surroundings.

Red-tipped tupelos

Off the Siasconset Road

Dwarf sumac

Red cedar, scarlet tupelo, bayberry. On the way to Wauwinet

A milkweed seed floats from its pod

The moors in mid-October

The Shawkemo hills

The great cranberry bog

OPPOSITE: Long Pond, from Massasoit

Looking toward Polpis Harbor from Pocomo Head